NATURALISM AND CRITICISM

To Renate and Gita

NATURALISM AND CRITICISM

by

R. A. MALL

MARTINUS NIJHOFF – THE HAGUE – 1975

ISBN 90 247 1739 6

PRINTED IN THE NETHERLANDS

CONTENTS

PREFACE

The present work is the product of several years study of the various aspects of Kant's Critical Philosophy and Hume's naturalism. During that time many individuals have helped with this work and it is hardly possible to set down the names of all of them. One name does deserve special mention – Prof. Dr. H. Heimsoeth with whom the author has discussed some of the very knotty problems of Kantian Philosophy.

Although Hume has been – as Kant freely admits in the Preface to his "Prolegomena" – one of the most decisive influences and turning points in the philosophical development of Kant, the author does not thematize in this work the age-old problem of whether Kant really read, understood and refuted Hume. That it has been, ever since Hume wrote, a favorite pursuit among philosophers to answer him, to refute him, and to refute Kant's attempt at refutation of him, irrespective of its being convincing or not, must be mentioned with special respect.

The "criticism" of Kant, ever since he developed it, has attracted more attention and received more sympathetic interpretations than the "naturalism" of Hume which has been neglected for quite a very long period. The present work hopes partly to do justice to this neglected aspect; it thematizes Kants criticism as well as Hume's naturalism as two independent and original "hypotheses" towards the solution of the ancient and very tangled problem of the relation between experience and reason, a problem which appears in many guises – rationalism, empiricism, dogmatism, scepticism, the a priori and the a posteriori.

The work is based on a particular understanding of criticism and of naturalism which is a middle path between dogmatic rationalism and dogmatic empiricism. This go-between character of criticism as well as naturalism leads us to our thesis that there is a programmatic and archetectonic similarity between Critical Philosophy (Kant) and naturalism (Hume). In order to substantiate this thesis the author undertakes a critical and comparative study of the principles of human nature (Hume) and the categories of understanding (Kant). The author's very sympathetic but not uncritical or orthodox interpretation of Kant's and Hume's philosophy shows that there is a foundational and fundamental relativity to the special constitution of human mind, human nature. This means that the fundamental principles of Kant's criticism as well as of Hume's naturalism rest on an ultimately factual foundation, to wit, the anthropocentric constitution of human nature. Thus, in the course of his interpretation the author has come to suggest and develop his theory towards "anthropocentrism" with regard to criticism and naturalism.

The programmatic similarity as suggested here must not be stretched too far, for that would involve artificial attempts at arbitrary philosophical interpretation. And the suggested theory of anthropocentrism has been sketched out very briefly; it needs further investigations and elaborations.

It would also be evident to a careful reader that the critical philosophy of Kant with its conceptual clarity and framework coupled with a tight terminological strategy surpasses in systematic topography Hume's naturalism which of course is very rich in original philosophical insights but poor in the systematization of them. Another undercurrent of the author's interpretation would also be clear to a careful reader – that the philosophical continuity from Hume onwards does not run so much via Kant but via Meinong, Brentano, James and Avenarius to Husserl.

The present study suffers from one great limitation, and this must be made clear in order to avoid any misconception about the author's intentions. The author has not sufficiently taken into account the other important aspects of Kantian as well as Humean philosophy, e.g. their epistemology, logic and morals. He has undertaken the humble task, first, of bidding farewell to the "too" much talked of problem regarding Kant's understanding of Hume and, second, of raising the entire discussion to a new platform.

R.A.M.

CHAPTER I

INTRODUCTION: HUME AND KANT
AND THE HISTORY OF IDEAS

One of the most tangled problems in the long history of philosophy is the problem of the relation between experience and reason, a problem which appears in many guises: rationalism vs. empiricism, idealism vs. realism, the a priori vs. the a posteriori, and the analytic vs. the synthetic. Almost all the attempts to overcome the opposition between these two concepts have ended more or less in either surrendering reason to experience or experience to reason. The present work thematizes this age-old problem anew with particular reference to Hume's "naturalism" and Kant's "criticism". Both Hume and Kant claim to have given to philosophy a new and sure foundation.

It is not an easy task to determine the place of Hume and Kant in the history of ideas, not only because both of them tread new ground but also because of an ambivalent relation of Kant to Hume. Kant is full of praise for Hume, but he also takes him to task for not being able to rescue the ship of philosophy from the deep sea of scepticism.[1]

The history of ideas shows clearly that the sciences dealing with man and his nature are primarily interested in working out a clear-cut map of human mental geography. The philosophies of Hume and Kant aim at such a fundamental and foundational science of man and his capacities to know, judge, feel and act. Thus the question regarding the relation between these two philosophies is of paramount importance not only from the point of view of the history of ideas but also from that of the philosophical problems.

There are a long range of philosophical attempts discovering Hume anew: logical positivism, naturalism, phenomenology, Deism, atheism etc. The Kantian discovery of Hume is one of the most influential, mainly due to the fact that continental thought, particularly German thought, discovered Hume via Kant. And the Kantian reading of Hume

---

[1] Cf. Kant: *Prolegomena*, Preface.

still persists in certain quarters although much has been written on Kant's misunderstanding of Hume.

The author is of the conviction that the traditional interpretation of Humean thought popularized by Reid and Beattie does not do justice to the philosophical spirit, intentions and achievements of his philosophy.[2] Compared to Reid and Beattie, Kant understands Hume far better and is more sympathetic to him.

Hume's philosophical teachings anticipated much which started bearing fruit from the time of Kant onward. Kant honestly confesses that ,,my recollection of David Hume's teaching (die Erinnerung des David Hume) was the very thing which many years ago first interrupted my dogmatic slumber, and gave my investigations in the field of speculative philosophy quite a new direction.''[3]

Hume's naturalism attempts to avoid the one-sidedness of sense (sensualism) and reason (rationalism). A similar intention lies also at the back of Kant's criticism. This means that there is a good programmatic similarity between these two philosophers. The main objective of the present work is a cooperative confrontation of Hume's naturalism with Kant's criticism. The programmatic similarity here hinted at needs further elaborations and the author would like to warn the reader not to stretch it too far lest it become artificial and break down.

Properly speaking, Hume is neither a follower of the Locke-Berkeley tradition nor just a precursor of Kant. In similarity with Kant's criticism, the most constructive part of Hume's philosophy is represented by his naturalism.[4]

Descartes is generally recognized to be the father of modern philosophy. Hume is a critic of Descartes no less than Kant is. Although Hume belongs on the whole to the tradition of empirical thought, still he is not blind to it. Since scepticism is not and cannot be a feasible philosophy of life, Hume rejects empiricism in so far as it entails such a philosophy. The real name of Humean empiricism is naturalism which rejects sensualistic empiricism as well as dogmatic rationalism.

Descartes, according to Hume, belongs to the tradition of dogmatic rationalism. Hume is more diffident of his philosophical doubts as well as of his philosophical convictions and achievements than Descartes who recommends a method of universal doubt of all our principles, opinions and even our faculties. He reaches the most original and cer-

---

[2] Cf. R. A. Mall: *Hume's Concept of Man*, Chapters, I and II.
[3] N. K. Smith: *A Commentary to Kant's "Critique of Pure Reason,"* Introduction.
[4] Cf. C. W. Hendel: *Studies in the Philosophy of David Hume*, Chapter XI.

tain principle "cogito ergo sum". Hume comments on this: "But neither is there any such original principle which has a prerogative above others, that are self-evident and convincing: or if there were, could we advance a step beyond it ... The Cartesian doubt, therefore, were it ever possible to be attained by any human creature (as it plainly is not) would be entirely incurable ..."[5] The species of scepticism which Descartes in the eyes of Hume inculcates is termed by Hume "antecedent", for it is recommended prior to all study and philosophy.

In order to prove the veracity of our senses, Descartes introduces the concept of the supreme being, and this round-about way via God is entitled by Hume an "unexpected circuit". Thus, it is not the so-called original principle of Descartes but his God which rescues him from scepticism. Hume overturned the "philosophic card-castle erected by Descartes"[6] and it helps us in judging his place in the history of ideas. Hume maintains that the very Cartesian approach to solving philosophical problems is misguided because "if the external world be once called in question, we shall be at a loss to find arguments, by which we may prove the existence of that Being or any of his attributes."[7] Hume thus also criticizes the ontological argument for the existence of God.

Although Kant could not read Hume's "Enquiries" in full and failed to see that Hume's declaration of the soul as a bundle can be understood as a strong reaction against the Cartesian theory of the same, still a similar criticism is levied by Kant against Descartes. According to Kant, Cartesian idealism is "problematic" for it takes the empirical assertion "I am" to be beyond all doubt.[8] Kant is much more similar to Hume in his criticism of the Cartesian argument for the existence of God. The point of departure for Hume as well as for Kant is that existence is no predicate.

Locke's consciousness as a *tabula rasa* has at its disposal two sources of knowledge: sensation and reflection. But all that is directly given to us are the ideas as copies of the objects and not the objects themselves. Thus Locke is led to accept the correspondence theory of truth and tries to compare the original with its representation. But the original is known to us only through the ideas which represent it. This further compels Locke to utter that well-known sentence: 'the substance is I

<hr>

[5] D. Hume: *Enquiries Concerning the Human Understanding and Concerning the Principles of Morals*, pp. 149–50.
[6] B. Willey: *The Eighteenth Century Background*, p. 110.
[7] D. Hume: *Enquiries*, p. 153.
[8] I. Kant: *Kritik der reinen Vernunft*, p. 272, (B 274).

know not what'. Hume criticizes Locke not only for his loose use of the term "ideas" but mainly for his inconsequent thinking. Locke wants to be both at the same time: an empiricist as well as a rationalist.

Berkeley, Hume further comments, boasts to have avoided the troubles of Locke. In the opinion of Berkeley, Locke got into trouble mainly because he accepted the material substance. Thus, the remedy Berkeley proposes is that we should accept only the human consciousness and its ideas, and that which we generally term matter is nothing but a cluster of ideas. Berkeley offers the epistemological explanation for this position through his theory of *esse est percipi*. Thus, he is led to his well-known subjective idealism which is entitled by Kant as "dogmatic idealism".

But the victory of Berkeley over Locke is an illusion because he fails to make room for his notion of God in his famous theory of *esse est percipi*. In order to rescue the external world Berkeley reverses the relation between human mind and God. In the absence of human perception, things do exist in and through the perception of God. Berkeley who composed his book "Three Dialogues between Hylas and Philonous in Opposition to Sceptics and Atheists" is called by Hume the father of modern scepticism.[9]

Kant, to begin with, admires Locke for his attempts to work out a particular physiology of human understanding.[10] But soon Kant takes Locke to task for his misguided attempt to even derive the categories of understanding from our experience. Any attempt at an empirical deduction of the categories is a nightmare to Kant.

Kant, as well as Hume, charges Locke with inconsequence. And both of them argue in a very similar way: that which transcends the limits of empirical experience cannot be derived from it. So far, Hume and Kant seem to fulfil a very similar function in the process of the development of modern philosophy through their criticism of the Cartesian philosophy on the one hand and of the philosophies of Locke and Berkeley on the other.

But this so-called functional similarity of the roles of Hume and Kant in the history of ideas breaks down when they proceed to work out a constructive philosophy of their own to meet the challenge coming from their own criticisms of the philosophies of their predecessors.

Kant is right in reading Hume the message of a "new science of

---

⁹ Hume writes: "... and indeed most of the writings of that very ingenious author [Berkeley] form the best lessons of scepticism ..." (*Enquiries*, p. 155).
¹⁰ I. Kant: *Kritik der reinen Vernunft*, Preface to the first edition.

man". But he fails to see that Hume's naturalism represents this new foundational science. This is the root cause of Kant's misunderstanding of Hume's philosophy. Since Kant saw in Hume only a critical genius who proposes no solution of his own, he never attempted any critical appreciation of Hume's "naturalism." Thus the central claim of Kant's critical philosophy, to have successfully solved the Humean problem, can be discussed at two different levels and from two different angles of vision: (i) wherein lies Hume's own solution of the philosophical problems and (ii) how this can be compared, opposed and confronted with that of Kant's. To throw some light on this neglected aspect of the Hume-Kant relationship is one of the main aims of this work. Besides, it also aims at showing the independent character of Hume's naturalism which in certain aspects might be less comprehensive and less clear than Kant's criticism, but it is in no way less modern. The modern "hypothetical realism,"[11] which is based on a natural history of human knowledge, maintains that the so-called thought-necessities are in fact "native" – native to the very organization we call human biology and physiology. Such a reading of human knowledge is nearer to the insights of Hume than to those of Kant.

It is commonplace in philosophy to remark about the mysterious relation of Kant to Hume. But such remarks have failed to be fruitful mainly because the majority of philosophers interested in this problem started with the presupposition that Hume had no positive solution of his own. This so-called mysterious character of the relation between these two philosophers is due largely to the commentators, and Kant is not fully blameless. In his major work "Critique of Pure Reason", Kant repeatedly refers to Hume and his indebtedness to him but he consistently fails to notice the positive side of Hume's philosophy.

Kant is happy and satisfied to learn from the philosophical mistakes of Hume which, as Kant understands Hume, are full of hints. Kant's job is to work out these hints which he performs in the name of his critical philosophy.

The main mistake of Hume in the eyes of Kant is that Hume, although a far more critical philosopher than all his predecessors, errs in attempting to deduce the concepts of the understanding from experience. This is nothing, Kant further maintains, but denying the existence of the categories, which means to fall into scepticism. Kant was strengthened in his opinion of Hume by his further firm conviction

---

[11] Cf. K. Lorenz: *Die Rückseite des Spiegels. Versuch einer Naturgeschichte menschlichen Erkennens,* pp. 15 ff.

that there is only one type of deduction of the categories, namely the transcendental deduction.

Kant of course falsely attributed Hume to have undertaken an empirical deduction. Hume very clearly denies and criticizes the line of argument according to which experience can be the sole ground of the principles of nature. Thus, Kant fails to differentiate Hume from "Hume".

As far as I have been able to determine, there are two theories about the relationship between Hume and Kant: (i) Kant successfully solved the problem of Hume and (ii) Kant failed to do so.[12]

The general tendency among philosophers is to label Kant as a protagonist of the principle of causality and Hume as an antagonist. Hume unlike Kant denies the existence of the world and of the soul. But a deeper and consistent understanding of Hume's philosophy shows us that he is as much a protagonist of the causal principle as Kant. It is Kant and not Hume, as Husserl has shown, who fails to thematize the world. The main difference between Hume and Kant lies not so much in whether they accept a system of principles as well as categories but more in showing the whereabouts of these principles and categories. Unlike Kant, Hume is not interested in a formal-transcendental deduction of the categories, for that would really mean relegating the whole problem to the field of the relations of ideas. Hume derives the undoubted certainty, necessity and universality of his principles from the original propensities of human nature. In a letter to Stewart, Hume once more clarifies his meaning on this point: "But allow me to tell you, that I never asserted so absurd a proposition as that anything might arise without a cause: I only maintained that our certainty of the Falsehood of that proposition proceeded neither from Intuition nor Demonstration, but from another source."[13] This "another source" is one of the central themes of Hume's naturalism.

Like Kant, Hume too is eager to find principles which help explain the coming to be of human experience. The different principles of human nature are functionally parallel to the categories of the understanding in the philosophy of Kant. Like Kantian categories, the Humean principles are also constitutive of experience, but the Humean sense of constitution is quite different from the Kantian sense of it. In opposition to the Kantian sense, we may call the Humean sense "weak"

---

[12] Among the notable English commentators, N. K. Smith belongs to the second group while Paton belongs to the first.

[13] Quoted by N. K. Smith: *The Philosophy of David Hume*, p. 413.

because the principles, unlike Kantian categories, do not determine the nature of all (possible) experience for all time to come. There is not a rigid line of demarcation between experience and reason. Hume's insight that there is no dichotomy between experience and reason is fully worked out in Husserl's phenomenology.[14]

In opposition to the Humean weak sense of constitution, Kant's sense of it may be termed "strong". This further leads to a different understanding of the concept of the "a priori" in the philosophies of Hume and Kant. The a priori of Kant is very rigid whereas the a priori of Hume points towards the propensities of human nature that have a reciprocal relation to human experience.

It follows from what has been said above that Hume and Kant are two very important figures in the history of ideas. This is true not only because of their very critical attitude towards sensualistic empiricism and dogmatic rationalism, but mainly because their philosophies represent two very similarly motivated but very differently worked out systems towards the solution of perennial philosophical problems.

The central problem of Kant's "Critique of Pure Reason" is: How are synthetic a priori judgments possible? That they are possible is for Kant beyond all doubt. The way Kant formulates this problem seems to point out that he was well acquainted with Hume's questioning of the very causal principle in his bigger work "Treatise", a quotation of which Kant happened upon while reading the German translation of Beattie's "Essay on the Nature and Immutability of Truth".

The character of Hume's "Treatise" is more radical and general than that of his "Enquiry". Hume's main teaching regarding the universal principle of causality is that it is of non-rational character. It is also not self-evident. Since it does not belong to the field of the relations of ideas it is beyond all demonstrations. But still it is a necessary principle and is of utmost need as a principle of organization of experience. The only way to explain it is to interpret it as a manner in which our "propensities" work when they come in contact with other objects. This is the naturalistic explanation of the causal principle. Hume says: "Nature has determined us to judge as well as to breathe and feel."[15]

This naturalistic standpoint of Hume attacks not only the rationalists who claim to demonstrate the principles (categories) but also the empiricists who try to establish them on the grounds of induction from experience. Thus, the causal inference is not inductive inference.

---

[14] Cf. R. A. Mall: *Experience and Reason*, Chapters IX, X and XI.
[15] D. Hume: *Treatise*, p 183

The most central teaching of Hume is that our inferences lack not only demonstrative but also inductive proofs. It is our natural beliefs which lie at the back of our inferences. Induction, thus, according to Hume, is a non-rational process.

Kant is very much in agreement with Hume, for he too is convinced of the synthetic character of the causal principle. But he completely disagrees with Hume's questioning of the a priori character of this principle. This is what troubled Kant when he first read Hume. Kant's dilemma is: if Hume is right then the established sciences like physics and mathematics are impossible. And if he is wrong we have to show the possibility of the synthetic a priori judgments. Kant thinks that Hume has failed to universalize his problem. But we know that Hume is talking not only of the contingency of the concrete causal inferences but he is also questioning the very causal axiom. Thus, Hume is asking not only about how a priori knowledge is possible but also about how experience is possible. If we bear this in mind and maintain that Kant was awakened by Hume to both these problems, much that is obscure in Kant's critical philosophy becomes clear.

CHAPTER II

SENSE, REASON AND IMAGINATION

The crucial problem Hume puts to himself is that between the two extreme positions of sensualistic empiricism and dogmatic rationalism a third position must be found which might do full justice to the non-sceptical and non-speculative philosophical intentions of his philosophy. In other words, Hume is in search of a common root which is related to the senses on the one hand and to reason on the other. Imagination is this common root between the opposing poles of sense and reason.

Before Hume introduces his own theory of imagination, he very clearly shows in his "Treatise" that sense as well as reason, if left to themselves, lead to scepticism and dogmatism. Thus, his own theory of imagination is called upon to solve the problem arising out "of scepticism with regard to the senses" and "of scepticism with regard to reason".[1]

Hume's scepticism with regard to the senses occurs when he tries to scrutinize the senses as one of the main sources of our belief in the existence of the external world, causality and so on. There is no rational remedy to the reasoning of a sceptic, who no doubt "believes" but continues to doubt and reason about his belief. Thus, the free play of scepticism is the cancellation of reason by reason. The only result of sceptical argumentation is momentary amazement and confusion. Since a sceptic fails to defend his reason by reason, he also fails to produce any conviction.

Hume is very particular in clearly telling us that his is not the Cartesian way of doubting the existence of the external world. "We may well ask", he writes, "*What causes induce us to believe in the existence of body*? but 'tis in vain to ask, *Whether there be body or not*?"[2] That there are bodies is a point which is not only beyond all doubt but which must

---

[1] Cf. D. Hume: *Treatise*, Book I, Part IV.
[2] *Ibid.*, p. 187.

also be taken for granted in all our reasonings. Hume is more Husserlian than Cartesian or Kantian in his approach to the problem of the external world.[3]

What casuses induce us then to believe in the existence of body? In his attempt to find an adequate answer to this fundamental question, Hume thematizes our senses. He first points out that there is a general confusion among philosophers stemming from their being unable to clearly distinguish between the reason "why we really attribute a continued existence to objects even in the absence of our perception of them" and the reason "why we suppose that these objects are distinct from our mind and its perceptions". In other words, the first question deals with the problem of the independent existence of the objects while the second question thematizes the problem of the nature of these objects. Since these two questions are two sides of the same coin, any answer to either of them will imply an answer to the other. Hume thus asks whether the fundamental belief regarding the independent and continued existence of the objects is produced by the senses, reason or imagination.[4]

When our senses stop to operate they cannot continue to operate, and, thus, for this reason they cannot be the real source of our belief in the continued existence of objects. Since Hume has already done away with Berkeley's God, in whose perceptions these objects might continue to exist, he resolves that the senses cannot be said to produce the idea of an independent and continued existence. From all this, Hume concludes that the opinion of a continued and independent existence can never arise from our senses. This is what he means by his phrase "scepticism with regard to the senses".

If we make our senses the last court of appeal regarding the problem of a continued and independent existence, we would utterly fail to come to any belief because all our perceptions are the same in the manner of their existence. Our sense-perceptions are all transitory; and the picture of the world that logically emerges on the basis of these perceptions must be transitory in nature, too. To put it in the more modern terminology of sense-data philosophy: sensations and perceptions are always changing. They furnish us only with fragmentary data of a particular table. We are directly "acquainted" not with the object "table" but with the sense-data of an "X". Thus, the real object "table" becomes a construction.

---

[3] Cf. R. A. Mall: *Experience and Reason*, Chapter VII.
[4] Cf. D. Hume: *Treatise*, pp. 188 ff.

Hume also criticizes the view which equates perceptions with the objects perceived. So long as we argue on the basis of such a theory of perception we can never be able to infer the existence of the one from the other. Although Hume could not give a very satisfactory solution to the problem of perception, still he successfully avoided the idealistic position which suffers in some form or another from reductionism.

Coming to an examination of reason as a source of our belief in the continued and independent existence of objects, Hume places it in opposition to the senses. Reason is active and thus opposes the senses which are passive. The field of knowledge in which reason reigns supreme is the field of demonstrative knowledge, the field of the relations of ideas. Reason in this sense is considered by Hume as a kind of cause of which truth is the natural effect.[5]

Since reason can prove or disprove things only in the field of the relations of ideas and since the problem of a continued and independent existence of objects belongs to the field of the matters of fact, reason can be of no great help to us in deciding for the reason of our belief in the existence of the external world. And if we still apply this reason to this field of knowledge, knowledge would be degenerated to probability. And it is not probability but certainty which is the essence of our belief. Belief is different from fiction.[6]

But Hume does not conclude that a total scepticism is the only way open to us. The only cure against sceptical reason is nature, which has determined us to judge as well as to breathe and feel. And "whoever has taken the pains to refute the cavils of this *total* scepticism, has really disputed without an antagonist ..."[7]

Hume's main intention in discussing and disputing the claims of reason is to show the truth of his central hypothesis: "belief is more properly an act of the sensitive, than of the cogitative part of our natures."[8] If reason is allowed to take full control of our knowledge in the field of matters of fact, we would be at a loss to discover the different principles of nature which are the guiding principles not only in our epistemology but also in morals and religion.

It is interesting to see that Hume differentiates two very subtle shades of the same reason which are different in their operations and intentions. The sceptical and the dogmatical reason "are of the same

---

[5] Cf. *Ibid.*, pp. 180 ff.
[6] Cf. R. A. Mall: *Hume's Concept of Man*, pp. 62 ff.
[7] D. Hume: *Treatise*, p. 183.
[8] *Ibid.*

kind, tho' contrary in their operation and tendency". Hume describes the peculiar nature of their context. Since both of them are of equal force in the beginning they never lose in their encounter. "Were we to trust entirely to their self-destruction, that can never take place, 'till they have first subverted all conviction, and have totally destroyed human reason."[9]

Thus, Hume reaches the conclusion that neither our senses nor reason are in a position to give us any assurance regarding the continued and independent existence of the objects. And since the main object of our enquiry is not whether there are bodies or not but "how do we come to believe them", Hume turns to some other source of this belief. This belief, he says, is due to the most universal faculty of imagination. There is never a total suspension of our belief, because in an oblique manner our imagination works to produce the idea of a continued and independent existence along with the certainty of our belief. Our senses and reason are not only unable to produce it but also unable to destroy it.

One of the most original contributions of Hume's philosophy is to have shown that our whole conceptual world is the product of our imaginative faculty. And Kant, in this respect, is one who unknowingly carries the task still further and accomplishes it better than Hume. Kant was fully unaware of Hume's theory of imagination.

Hume develops his own theory of imagination step by step. He first shows the ambiguous character of the term "imagination". Its nature is vague and it is generally used in a double sense. As commonly understood, it stands for our ability to freely put ideas together and to separate them. Imagination is hardly distinguished from fancy. This first non-Humean use and sense of imagination is contrasted with memory. Imagination is freer than memory, for memory is always related to the past. In memory, the original order of our impressions and perceptions remains to a great extent intact. Thus, the degree of vivacity possessed by memory lies between that of impressions and ideas. In imagination, as opposed to memory, there is hardly any vivacity of our original impressions. "The faculty by which we repeat our impressions in the first manner (retaining a considerable degree of its first vivacity) is called *MEMORY* and the other the IMAGINATION."[10]

The other, the Humean sense of imagination, distinguishes it from fancy. Imagination, according to Hume's own view of it, is the very quality of our mind to enliven some ideas beyond others. And the ideas

[9] *Ibid.*, p. 187.
[10] *Ibid.*, pp. 8–9.

thus enlivened by imagination are believed to be in opposition to the *mere* ideas which are produced by our fancy and lack this quality. "The memory, senses and understanding are, therefore, all of them founded on the imagination, or the vivacity of our ideas."[11]

For such a sudden change in the meaning of the term "imagination", Hume gives his own reason and justification. In the imagination he distinguishes between the permanent, irresistible and universal principles and the principles which are changeable, weak and irregular. Customary transition from causes to effects and from effects to causes belongs to the first sense of imagination. The universality of the principle of causality is thus grounded in the universality of the human imagination.

The importance of the first sense of imagination is so great that its removal might mean the destruction of human nature as such.[12] This means that Hume is convinced of the unavoidable character of imagination in the workings of our life. Hume recommends this sense of the imagination to the serious philosophers.

Those, including Kant, who see in Hume simply a sensualistic treatment of the principle of causality fail to realise the importance of this very fundamental distinction made by Hume.

It is this view of imagination which is contrasted with the concept of imagination as it has been used by the ancient as well as modern philosophers in producing fictions like substance and accident and the difference between primary and secondary qualities. The cause for all these misguided inferences, Hume argues, is that these philosophers base their reasonings on principles which are neither universal nor unavoidable in human nature.

The dual character of imagination (in Kantian terminology: the productive and the reproductive nature of our imagination) becomes clearer when Hume goes on to oppose it with the senses and with reason. Compared to the sense, imagination is the faculty which is less lively but which works at a deeper level in human nature. Its ideas are vivid and it is this vivacity which brings it nearer to the senses. Opposed to reason, imagination is the very source of the different principles of custom, habit and belief. Herein lies the greatest importance of imagination, and that means that the different principles of nature are not rational constructions of our reason. It is this concept of ima-

11 *Ibid.*, p. 265.
12 *Ibid.*, p. 225.

gination which bridges the gap between the two otherwise very rival sources of our knowledge: the senses and reason.

Opposed to phantasy, imagination is the principle of a vivid "postulation", of an anticipation and continuation. If we examine the problem of a continued existence, we find that the objects to which we attribute such an existence are marked out by *constancy, regularity* and *coherence*. Since Humean imagination possesses such qualities of regularity and coherence, it comes to our help in that it allows us to "conceive" a more regular, constant and coherent world than that which is delivered either by our senses or reason. The piecemeal knowledge we have of the world needs to be supplemented. Imagination fulfils this function of supplementation and allows us to believe in the continued and independent existence of the external world and other objects.

Our knowledge involves the problem of transcendence which is also epistemological in nature. Imagination, being the reservoir of *unsensed sensibilia*, solves this problem of epistemological transcendence by functioning as the faculty of anticipation, supplementation and continuation. Imagination is, thus, a method, a plan of procedure endowed with the function of co-ordination. Such a phenomenological interpretation of the concept of imagination leaves the question of an ontological status of imagination fully open.

Without the supplementary co-ordination of our imagination, the fragmentary or gappy data of sensations cannot give rise to the opinion of a continued and independent existence. "To use this method", Price writes, "is a fundamental tendency in human nature; and the activity in which we use it is called by Hume 'Imagination'."[13]

This function of supplementary co-ordination is no problem of truth or falsity, since it formulates no proposition. Thus, to ask whether this procedure is true or false is senseless and amounts to asking whether respiration or digestion is true or false.

From what has been said above, we may note down the main functions of imagination: *supplementation* and *synthetization* (co-ordination). Hume lays more stress on the first and less on the second.

Imagination provides us, to use an expression of Price, with the *grammer of material objects*; for in order to understand material objects as complete objects we need the help of our imagination. It is imagination which leads us from *part perception* to *whole perception*. This very phenomenological sense of imagination teaches us that the objects of

13 H. H. Price: *Hume's Theory of the External World*, p. 195.

perceptions do continue to exist even without their being always perceived by our senses.

Of course, we always notice some degree of regularity in our perceptions, but Hume is keen to point out that this perceived regularity alone can never be the sole foundation to infer a greater regularity in objects not perceived, for that would imply a contradiction, viz. a habit, as Hume says, "acquired by what was never present to the mind." Since this extending of our reasoning beyond the perceptions can never be the direct effect of habit, there must be some other principle of more authority and weight. And we know "that the imagination, when set into any train of thinking is apt to continue, even when its object fails it, and like a galley put in motion by the oars, carries on its course without any new impulse."[14]

The faculty of imagination is at work when we infer causes from effects and vice versa. We have observed: the stone fell down and the glass was broken. Now seeing the stone and the glass again, we imagine first the falling down of the stone and then the breaking of the glass. It is this act of imagining that must be performed before we talk of any causal relation. But this does not mean that Hume starts from the particular causality to reach the general causality. The general causal principle is not abstracted from the particular causal principles. The universality of the causal principle has nothing to do with particular temporal and spatial relations. It is the universality of our mental disposition (propensities).

The opinion of the vulgar consciousness that objects exist when not perceived may be illogical and unfounded, but this is the most natural attitude to human mind. This is also the attitude that is recommended by our imagination. Nay, it is due to the imagination.[15]

The main purpose which Hume's theory of imagination serves is to answer how we come to believe in the independent and continued existence of objects. Imagination has the power to transpose and change ideas; it extends reasoning beyond the perceptions. It is the main source of general principles. It is the principle that completes an imperfect uniformity. Hume contrasts imagination with memory, with reason, with sense, with experience, judgment and understanding, for it is the ground on which all of them are founded.

Kant in his critical philosophy is faced with a similar dilemma: to find out a medium between the senses and understanding (reason). And

---

[14] D. Hume: *Treatise*, p. 198.
[15] Cf. N. K. Smith: *The Philosophy of David Hume*, p. 488.

imagination is this common ground, related on the one hand with the sensibility and on the other with the understanding.

The most fundamental assumption made by Kant is that judging and perceiving are different from each other and that any attempt to reduce the one to the other is a philosophical error of far reaching consequences. The two antagonistic theories of empiricism and rationalism are such reductions.

Judging and perceiving are two distinct faculties of the mind – understanding and the senses. Sense is the medium through which objects are given to us; understanding is the faculty by means of which they are thought. Perceptions belong to the sense whereas concepts belong to the understanding.[16]

The notion that all, or nearly all, general concepts are a posteriori in character is the very thesis of empiricism, and Hume and Kant repudiate this thesis when they show in their own ingenious ways that concepts cannot be traced back to mere sense-perceptions. Causality as a kind of *necessary* connection cannot be derived from the contingent perceptions. And this means that it is an a priori concept – a concept of our understanding. The a priori concepts, according to the critical philosophy, do not describe the objects (this is the job of a posteriori concepts), instead they order the materials (the mannifold) given to us through the sense. Thus, the application of a priori concepts really transforms our perceptions in such a way that a new product comes to be. This new product is what we call knowledge. It is this insight Kant's which he mentions in his letter to his friend Marcus Herz and which essentially is his *Copernican revolution or hypothesis* according to which the objects are made to confirm to the concepts and not vice versa. Thus the main job of the critical philosophy is to consider the a priori constituents of knowledge. In other words, the question that Kant puts to himself is how synthetic a priori judgments are possible.

In attempting to solve the problem of knowledge from a new stand point different from and opposed to both sensualistic empiricism and dogmatic rationalism, Kant examines the different sources of knowledge. These sources are sensibility and understanding. The sense is the faculty of intuition, i.e. it intuits objects or objects affect our senses. Sensibility is thus the capacity to obtain representation (Vorstellung) through the twin modes of space and time. Like Hume, Kant too postulates the existence of independent objects which affect our senses.

---

[16] Cf. I. Kant: *Kritik der reinen Vernunft*, B. 33.

Since object and intuition mutually imply each other, sensibility is the source both of object and intuition. Through intuition we apprehend object. Sensibility is opposed to spontaneity, but as the faculty of intuition it has its own a priori forms – space and time.

Reason, in the wider sense of the term, stands for the faculty of thought (understanding). Thus, reason and understanding (Verstand) may, in this loose sense, represent the same thing. This is opposed to sensibility and possesses spontaneity which sensibility lacks. The function of understanding is to think, to order, to *spell* (buchstabieren) the chaotic manifold of the senses. As the faculty of judgment, understanding is active and is the reservoir of the categories which are needed if the raw material supplied by our senses can be ordered so as to give birth to knowledge (Erkenntnis).

Knowledge is thus a product like the cooked food that needs not only the raw material but also the active art of cooking. Kant's epistemology is a treatise on this art of cooking. Since senses can only see (intuit) but cannot judge (order), in contrast to understanding which can judge but cannot intuit, Kant is urgently in need of a third instance which can play the role of a mediator between these two opposite poles of knowledge. It is this third instance which is called imagination in Kant's critical philosophy.

Programmatically, it is the same task which imagination takes over in Hume's as well as in Kant's philosophy – the task of mediation between reason and the sense. Before imagination can be scrutinized with regard to its ability to fulfill this function, the prerequisites for such a mediation must be made clear. Any instance which can take over the job of mediation must be such that it is related on the one hand to the senses and on the other to reason or understanding. It must bear resemblance to both of them without being reducible to either of them.

The imagination is not just phantasy. In its wider sense, it is the ability to represent objects even when they are not present to the senses. Kant distinguishes between two types of imagination: the reproductive and the productive. The *reproductive* imagination combines the representations according to the laws of association. The *productive* imagination combines the representations according to the laws of our understanding, i.e. to our categories.

Imagination in fact belongs to sensibility, with the main difference that it is able to *perceive* objects not present to the senses. The job of the productive imagination is to produce the badly needed synthesis which is not of empirical character. Imagination performs this function by subsuming the manifold of our sensation under the forms of understanding. Thus, imagination takes over the role of a mediator between sense and understanding. Before we count five and ten mangoes together, we do it in imagination. The real mechanism by which imagination works is described by Kant in the chapter on "Schematism".[17]

In all subsumption of an object under a concept, the representation of the first must resemble that of the second. In other words, the concept must include the object which has to be subsumed under the same concept. This task of Kant's critical philosophy is made more difficult because of the dissimilarity between the categories and the empirical concepts.

Kant, very much like Hume, is convinced that there must be such an instance which would execute this representation of the one in the other.[18] That which fulfils this function is Kant's transcendental *schema*.

The term "schema" stands for a procedure which enables us to realise the content of our concepts through the substitution of a more general representation. The transcendental schema is not a picture (Bild) but a rule (Regel). In order to show how such a schema works, Kant takes the help of time which is the formal condition of the manifold of the inner sense. In the pure intuition of time, there is a manifold a priori. This transcendental determination of time is similar to the categories in so far as it is general (allgemein) and is based upon an a priori rule. It is also similar to the appearance (Erscheinung) in so far as the time is necessarily implied in each and every empirical representation of the manifold. Thus, it is this transcendental time-determination (transzendentale Zeitbestimmung) which makes a successful mediation between sense and understanding possible.

With regard to the picture-character of the transcendental schema, Kant says: when I put on paper five dots one after the other, the result is a picture of the number five. But when I think of a number as such (which could be five or 100), I never get a particular picture of a particular number. It is rather a representation of a method, of a procedure which must be distinguished from the concrete picture as such. This general representation resulting from the application of a general procedure of imagination is termed schema by Kant. Since this method can be applied in the case of each particular concept, there corresponds a schema to every concept.[19]

<hr>

[17] I. Kant: *Kritik der reinen Vernunft.*
[18] Cf. *ibid.*, pp. 197 ff.
[19] Cf. *ibid.*, pp. 199 ff.

Imagination, Kant clearly maintains, lies very deep in our souls and is a hidden art (verborgene Kunst). It works at a subconscious level and guides all other types of syntheses. Understanding cannot be said to be unconscious of its activities. Since understanding, according to Kant, is the very faculty whereby the *a priori* is brought to consciousness, Kant must find another faculty capable of performing the above mentioned activities. He chooses the name "productive imagination" for such a faculty. The empirical reproductive processes do not exhaust the entire domain of imagination. Imagination is also capable of *transcendental* activities. Its pure transcendental synthesis belongs to this dimension of its nature.

Kant was troubled with the question that, if understanding is distinct and separate from imagination, how does it come that imagination acts just in the manner which is required to produce experience. In other words, Kant must explain the co-operation between imagination and understanding. Why imagination should work in this manner cannot be explained, but that it acts in such a manner explains the *de facto* existence of experience.

Since Kant cannot completely ignore the kinship between imagination and understanding, he goes so far as to identify them and to speak of understanding as imagination which has become self-conscious.[20] Elsewhere he says that they are distinct and separate. The mediating role of imagination can be explained only from the second point of view.

Kant has been criticized much for the artificiality his schematism involves. Whatever might be the drawbacks of his theory of imagination, it very well suits the purpose it is called upon to serve. The critical philosophy of Kant demands such an instance, which should explain the *de facto* character of our experience. Without imagination we cannot pass beyond the momentary sense-data and the phenomenon of knowledge could not be explained. Thus, the question of why imagination acts in such a manner cannot be asked, for it stands for a procedure.

No knowledge is possible without synthesis. And since this synthesis cannot be produced by our senses and reason, there must be imagination to do it. So far, Hume and Kant are much in agreement. The difference starts when Kant develops a very rigid system of the categories in opposition to the more flexible system of Hume's principle. The two questions, how we come to know objects and what is necessarily involved in knowing objects, must of course be kept separate. Kant claims to have given the final answer to the second question. But he

[20] Cf. *ibid.*, B. 162.

fails to see that even the forms of knowledge may come to be understood and interpreted as resulting from the natural history of human progress. Hume is less rigid on this point and that is what gives him a more modern look.

Comparing the Humean view of imagination with that of Kant, we discover not only programmatic and functional similarities between them but also other resemblances which relate to the very nature of this faculty.

Hume's distinction between the two types of imagination is very similar to the Kantian distinction between the empirical and the transcendental view of imagination. It is not out of place to remark that the Humean theory of the external world bears close resemblances to that of the Kantian theory of the phenomenal world. The sham and very shaky explanations given for our belief in the existence of the other objects are no longer acceptable. Hume and Kant, both have clearly shown in what way the theories of rationalism and empiricism err. We cannot think of Humean epistemology without the fundamental contributions made by imagination. The same applies to Kant.

In the very introduction of his *Treatise*, Hume speaks of his philosophical intentions, which sound very Kantian: "There is no question of importance", he writes, "whose decision is not compris'd in the science of man; and there is none, which can be decided with any certainty, before we become acquainted with that science. In pretending, therefore, to explain the principles of human nature, we in effect *propose a compleat system of the sciences, built on a foundation almost entirely new*,[21] and the only one upon which they can stand with any security."[22]

Price very aptly terms this philosophical intention of Hume "a Scottish version of Kant's Copernican revolution"[23] – Hume as well as Kant declares the human mind to be the real seat of knowledge. Thus, the Humean hint towards the problem of reality has been explicitly worked out by Kant.

Quite similar to Hume's programme above, Kant speaks in the Preface to his "Critique of Pure Reason" of a "Gerichtshof" (law court) which must be set up in order to decide the problems of philosophy.[24]

The way we have interpreted Hume's theory of imagination is not only of central importance to his own philosophical achievements, it

---

[21] Authors emphasis.
[22] D. Hume: *Treatise*, Introduction.
[23] H. H. Price: *Hume's Theory of the External World*, p. 9.
[24] Cf. I. Kant: *Kritik der reinen Vernunft*, Preface.

also anticipates much that finds its fullest expression in the Kantian solution of the problem of knowledge and experience. Kant in his famous letter to Moses Mendelssohn refers to this very problem, for whose solution he spent nearly twelve years of hard labor and reflection. At an early age, when he was about twenty-five, Hume raised the self-same problem.

The question regarding the ultimate nature of imagination is answered neither by Hume nor by Kant. Both of them accept its presence because they need such an instance of mediation between sense and reason.

Inspite of all these similarities there are differences which must not be overlooked. Hume's theory of imagination differentiates from Kant's because Hume emphasizes the *supplemental* character of imagination more than its *synthetic* character. Although both accept the phenomenal world to be in some sense a *construction*, Hume fails to deal with the problem of imagination in its transcendental dimension. The reason might lie in their temperamental difference which was itself motivated at least partly by their different philosophical backgrounds. The practical and pragmatic side of imagination is worked out by Hume more than by Kant who was interested mainly in the transcendental theory of imagination. Since Hume was against speculation as a fruitful method in philosophy, he never took the help of a purely formal-transcendental logic which Kant utilized to the fullest in working out the transcendental system of his philosophy.

CHAPTER III

HUME'S "PRINCIPLES" AND KANT'S "CATEGORIES[1]"

One of Hume's and Kant's most central claims is to have proposed and worked out a new system of thought which solves the age-old baffling problems of philosophy in an entirely new way. The "principles" of human nature which Hume discovers in his philosophy correspond programmatically to the "categories" which Kant works out in his philosophy. The thesis to be defended here is that the principles as well as the categories rest ultimately on the special constitution of human mind, human nature. The relativization of all our knowledge in every field of our enquiry to human nature is the central teaching of Hume's as well as of Kant's philosophy.

That there is no unanimity among philosophers regarding the Kantian answer to the Humean problem might well appear very disparaging to the history of philosophy.[2] No refutation of Hume is convincing although it has been a pious intention among metaphysicians and philosophers to refute Hume ever since he wrote.[3] Not only that, there is hardly any common understanding of what Hume's main problem was.[4] So long as Hume is studied with the intention to refute him we can hardly do justice to him and to his philosophy.

Hume is not only a destructive philosopher who ruthlessly pushes the Locke-Berkeley tradition to its solipsistic consequences and destroys the phantastic card-castle erected by Descartes, but also he is a philosopher putting forth a constructive system of the principles of human nature. This means that we must distinguish between the "official" and the "real" philosophy of Hume. The official reading of Hume over-

---

[1] This chapter is an enlarged re-edition of my paper "Humes Prinzipien-und Kants Kategoriensystem" originally published in Kant-Studien, 1971.

[2] Cf. E. W. Schipper: *Kant's Answer to Hume's Problem*, Kant-Studien, 1961–62.

[3] Cf. B. Russell: *History of Western Philosophy*, p. 634.

[4] Cf. E. Husserl: *Krisis der europäischen Wissenschaften und die transzendentale Phäno-menologie*, pp. 99 ff.

rates the importance of his sceptical thinking. This results in a one sided view of his philosophy: Hume as a sceptic, solipsist as well as the father of phenomenalism and atomistic positivism. The real philosophy of Hume grows out of his criticism of sensualistic empiricism and dogmatic rationalism. He proposes a philosophy of human nature which, without being transcendental, works out the main guiding principles of human mind. It is this science of man which Hume so clearly speaks of in the very opening pages of his "Treatise". "In pretending, therefore", he writes, "to explain the principles of human nature, we in effect propose a compleat system of the sciences, built on a foundation almost entirely new, and the only one upon which they can stand with any security."[5] Kant in his introduction to his "Critique of Pure Reason" also proposes a new fundamental science which he compares with Copernican revolution.

Hume's treatment of the causal problem aroused Kant from his dogmatic slumber. But there is a difference between Hume's treatment of this problem in his bigger work "Treatise" and in his "Enquiry". The first work is more radical and thematizes the very causal principle (axiom) whereas in the "Enquiry" Hume is interested in dealing with the particular causal relations.

Kant seems to have never read Hume's "Treatise" in the original and in full, and he first came to know about Hume's questioning the validity of the universal causal principle through reading Beattie's "Essay on the Nature and Immutability of Truth". Before reading this essay by Beattie, Kant realized well the enigmatic character of all a priori knowledge. It is only that after reading Hume he became still more convinced of the very problematic character of all such principles which claim to be synthetic and a priori at the same time. This meant that Kant saw in Hume a challenging problem regarding the justification of all principles similar in nature and function to that of the causal principle. This is the Humean hint Kant speaks of in his work.[6]

Hume very clearly pointed out that the causal principle is neither self-evident nor can it be demonstrated. He nevertheless accepted the synthetic character of this principle. For him, the causal principle has a very important function to fulfil in our experience, for it is the very principle of organization of our experience. Kant is thus in complete agreement with Hume about the synthetic character of this principle of

---

⁵ D. Hume: *Treatise*, p. XX.
⁶ Cf. I. Kant: *Prolegomena*, Vorwort (Preface).

causality. Kant's dilemma arises when he tries to mediate between the Humean theory of the instrumental character and the Leibnizean theory of the self-legislative character of our thought. The naturalistic instrumental view of thought favored the synthetic character of our judgment but rejected its a priori claims whereas the self-legislative character of our thought favored the a priori character of our thought and rejected its synthetic claim.

Since Kant was fully convinced of the presence of judgments which are both synthetic and a priori at the same time, he went on to show their possibility.[7] That there are such judgments is a proposition he starts with. Herein lies one of the most fundamental differences of approach between Hume and Kant. Kant's solution to the problem of synthetic a priori judgments indirectly contains his answer to the problem of Hume. But we know that Hume is more radical than Kant on this point, for he asks whether there are such judgments. He of course does maintain that there are such judgments, the main divergence being that he supplies us with a different explanation and justification of the whole issue. This means that the principles of human nature point to an originally human solution of his own problems. Kant failed to guess that Hume had any solution of his own to offer.

It is uncommon to use the term "system" in characterizing the philosophy of Hume for he is generally taken to be one who is against system building in philosophy. But when here we talk of a system of the principles of human nature, all we mean is that Hume develops a theory of mental activity according to which experience is more than a mere bundle of isolated sensations and perceptions. Our knowledge contains passive as well as active moments, and the different principles of human nature represent the active side of our nature.

We understand by Humean principles the different performances of human nature in its active relationship to the world of things and beings. These performances are always at work and the job of a philosophy of human nature is to discover and work out these otherwise anonymous principles. Hume's system of the principles is guided by his firm conviction that these principles without being derived from experience are still very much suitable to experience. Since they help constitute our knowledge in the sense of being organizing principles they can be termed as the guiding and leading principles of human knowl-

---

[7] "Such is the problem that was Kant's troublous inheritance from his philosophical progenitors, Hume and Leibniz." (N. K. Smith: *A Commentary to Kant's "Critique of Pure Reason,"* Introduction, p. xxxiii).

edge and experience. It is clear from what has been said above that Hume does accept some sort of a priori but the a priori propositions are not absolute because they all are relative – they are relativized to the very original performances and workings of human mind.

What are these principles which Hume works out in his science of man? They are, as Hume says, the different principles of "custom", "habit", "practice", "belief", "imagination", "sympathy" and so on.[8] Hume emphasizes the central point, that human knowledge is not possible without the participation of these principles because in the absence of these principles our "experience becomes useless, and can give rise to no inference or conclusion."[9]

In working out the principles of human nature Hume presents a "critique of human experience" which shows not only the nature of human experience but also determines its limits. In every inference in the field of matters of fact we start from the presupposition that future would resemble the past. This very act of extending the past to the future cannot be accomplished if we remain within the boundary lines of past experience. Thus experience alone is not and cannot be the cause of inference. Hume in fact wants to show the anticipative character of inference in the field of matter of fact. Induction is thus neither purely logical nor empirical but rather "natural".

In his "Abstract"[10] Hume clearly maintains that inferences made from the past to the future are "suitable to past experience". But he questions the very foundation of our judgments regarding experience, and this is his main criticism of experience which follows from his theory of a critique of experience. In other words, Hume wants to know what authorizes human experience to judge that future would resemble the past. He asks, "What is the foundation of all conclusions from experience?" To answer that it is our past experience is questioned by Hume, for "as to past 'experience' it can be allowed to give 'direct' and 'certain' information of those precise objects only, and that precise period of time, which fell under its cognizance." Our mundane experience, to use a term of Husserlian phenomenology, is, according to Hume, not in a position to explain our inferences.

The main problem which Hume never fails to insist upon is: "But why this experience should be extended to future times, and to other

<hr>

[8] Cf. R. A. Mall: *Hume's Concept of Man*, Chapters IV, V,VI, VII.

[9] D. Hume: *Enquiries Concerning the Human Understanding and Concerning the Principles of Morals*, p. 38.

[10] Cf. D. Hume: "An Abstract of a Treatise of Human Nature," reprinted in *Hume-Theory of Knowledge*, ed. by Valden-Thomson, Edinburgh, 1951.

objects?"[11] It is obvious that Hume like Kant is busy in showing the validity of the principles of human nature. But in opposition to Kant, Hume is not searching for a "metaphysical deduction" of the principles. The deduction Hume would accept would also not be a formal-transcendental one, because that would be purely analytic and would mean that the principles should belong not to the field of matters of fact but to that of the relations of ideas. This difference between Hume and Kant can be traced back to their different philosophical backgrounds and attitudes. Hume is more of an empiricist than Kant and Kant is more of a rationalist than Hume.

Our inferences from the past to the future are thus neither intuitive nor demonstrative, and this means that they are neither sensuous nor purely formal-logical. But this does not mean that they are then just "probable", because these inferences are accompanied by a peculiar certainty of our belief which is nearer to the vivacity of our impressions and completely different from the fictions of our phantasy. Belief is characterized by an immediacy which is the original quality of our perceptions. That which we "believe in" must of course be "conceived" first. But "mere" conception is not belief, for belief is "more" than mere conception. What is this "more" which accompanies our belief and not our fiction? We can easily conceive of an animal having the head of a man and the body of a horse, but it is not in our power to believe it. Belief is a "firmer conception, or a faster hold, that we take of the object."[12] And this firmness, force and vivacity is not a quality of our conception but rather of the very way, *manner*, in which our mind conceives something. Thus, belief is not a movement from the object to the subject but vice versa. It is an activity of our mind. It is again this "manner" of our conception which renders realities more present to us than fictions. All we can maintain is that belief is something which is felt by the mind.[13]

Hume terms as "propensities" the active moments lying at the back of our synthesizing and organizing activities of the raw materials of our experience. These propensities give rise to different "dispositions" when they are "activated" by sensations and impressions. Thus, the Humean principles of human nature are of the nature of propensities and dispositions. And our human mind is endowed with these propensi-

[11] D. Hume: *Enquiries*, pp. 30 ff.
[12] D. Hume: *Treatise*, p. 627.
[13] Cf. D. Hume: *Enquiries*, p. 49.

ties. This is what we may term here as Hume's "theory of mental activity".

It is not our experience that explains and validates these principles; it is rather these principles that explain and justify our experience. Hume failed to systematize these "mental principles" in the fashion of Kant. Had Hume grouped these principles in the manner of Kant, "the result might well have been labeled a 'Table of Categories' for the propensities actually play a role quite similar to that of the categories in the Critique of Pure Reason."[14]

The principles of human nature as operations are independent of thought (discursive) and reasoning. These principles represent "the accurate anatomy of human nature"[15] and are the most certain and original principles which Hume wants to proceed upon. In opposition to Kant's transcendental categories, the principles are "natural" in the sense of "easy", "genuine" performances of our nature.

Turning to the "categories" of Kant, we may start with the fundamental problem (Hauptfrage) of his "Critique of Pure Reason": the problem of determining the limits of pure reason. The main question for Kant is not regarding the possibility of our very faculty of thought, but it is rather the question *what* and *how much* can our understanding as well as reason know without the help of our experience.[16]

The ultimate factual basis of all our knowledge is the very fact of our human mind, which is so constituted that it enters into whatever happens to be an object of our enquiry. The present work tries to argue that such a limitation specifically to human constitution is to be found not only in Hume but also in Kant.

Kant was fully convinced of the self-legislative character of our thought and this is the essence of his "rationalistic heritage". But Kant was also confronted with the crucial problem of how we really synthesize and organize the manifold of sensuous perception. This manifold must be brought in under the concepts of our understanding which help us spell them out. The human mind is thus the law giving factor; it is also the very seat of origin of the categories.

The categories of Kant stand for necessary functions of our understanding as the faculty of judgment. Without these functions we cannot organize the raw materials of our experience apprehended through the

---

[14] R. P. Wolf: "Hume's Theory of Mental Activity," reprinted in *Hume*, edited by V. C. Chappell, p. 127.

[15] D. Hume: *Treatise*, p. 263.

[16] Cf. I. Kant: *Kritik der reinen Vernunft*, A XVII.

twin forms of intuition – space and time. Kant very clearly says that our nature is so constituted that our intuition can never be other than sensible. It is the very mode in which we are affected by objects.[17]

Since the categories synthesize and organize this chaotic manifold into an object of experience, they represent the a priori conditions of the very possibility of our knowledge. Categories are therefore the transcendental conditions of our experience. The concepts of the understanding like the forms of sensibility represent subjective conditions of human nature. In contrast to the forms of sensibility which are subjective conditions of human intuition, categories are subjective conditions of human thought.[18]

Kant discovers the categories by reflecting on the fundamental forms of our thinking, of our judging. The pure understanding is the faculty of judgment comprised of different functions. Kant works out these different functions of the pure understanding in order to list the table of the categories. Once, with the help of the traditional logic, Kant has listed the logical forms of our judgment, he deduces his table of the categories from this table of the forms of judgments. The problem of the validation of the categories leads Kant to penetrate deep into the possibility of our knowledge. The fundamental basis of such a validating deduction is what Kant terms "the transcendental unity of apperception" and this unity lies in the very principle that all our cognitions must be accompanied by the reflexive indication of the "I think". This principle is limited only to the type of understanding we human beings possess. It is only our human understanding which needs a special act of synthesis of the manifold, for it has the power only to think and not to intuit. Like the principles of human nature, the categories must be accepted as given ultimates in our intercourse with the world of things and beings. The only explanation or rationalization for their presence is simply the fact of their presence. We have no other way to explain why we have them.[19]

Categories are only forms without any content. They have their seat in the subject (a priori) but they possess objective validity and function as the ground and presupposition of all possible experience. This is Kant's "critical transcendental theory" of the categories.

Neither Hume nor Kant maintain that we can have knowledge or experience without any subjective contribution. But there is a "must"

---

[17] Cf. *ibid.*, A 51; B. 75.
[18] Cf. *ibid.*, A 89; B. 122.
[19] Cf. *ibid.*, B. 145–46.

in the Kantian deduction of the categories which is very difficult to reconcile with the spirit of Humean philosophy. Hume in calling his guiding principles "natural" avoids the rigorous character of Kantian deduction which goes so far as to fix the very number of the categories.

Coming to the interesting question of the *a priori*, we may start with the remark that Hume as well as Kant accepts principles which guide and constitute experience. These principles are themselves not experiences for it is they which make experience possible. The central thesis of any a priori is that experience is more than the mere materials of experience.

To talk of a priori principles in the philosophy of David Hume, is not without risk, for he is generally taken to be against all apriorism. Following the *official* reading of Hume's philosophy there is a very patent sense of the term "a priori". The a priori is what reigns supreme in the field of the relations of ideas. A priori knowledge here is demonstrable and certain. Our reason can be considered as a cause of which truth in this field is a result. All the judgments in the field of the relations of ideas are analytic in character.

In opposition to the judgments in the field of the relations of ideas, the judgments in the field of matters of fact are of synthetic character. They are not a priori in nature. Were these judgments in the field of matters of fact a priori in the sense that there are a priori judgments in the field of the relations of ideas, we could not conceive the opposite of any matter of fact. But this does not mean that Hume maintains there is no certainty in the field of matters of fact. All Hume maintains is that the falsity of the opposite in the field of matters of fact cannot be shown along the same line we apply in judging the falsity of the judgments in the field of the relations of ideas.

That there is a sense in talking of a priori in the philosophy of Hume can be shown in the following way: Hume clearly maintains that the principles which guide and organize the materials of our experience are not themselves experiences. As propensities they make experience possible and consequently every organized experience presupposes these principles. It is in this and only in this sense that we can attribute to Humean principles the character of being a priori. The Humean a priori is, to use an expression of Husserl's, an "empirisch-gebundenes Apriori".[20]

The term "a priori" stands in the philosophy of Kant for that particular element in our knowledge which is independent of and prior to

<hr>

[20] E. Husserl: *Erfahrung und Urteil*, pp. 454 ff.

experience. It is because of such an element in human experience that Kant speaks of constitutive factors of experience. Categories are these constitutive factors. Universality and necessity are two marks of the Kantian a priori. Kant argues that since we have necessary and universal knowledge and since experience cannot give rise to such a knowledge we must possess a priori principles as presuppositions of experience. If we take away from our sensuous knowledge all that is due to the manifold, there still remain certain a priori forms and concepts which *formally* determine the nature and scope of experience. Thus, in opposition to the Humean "empirically bound" a priori, Kant's a priori is formal, transcendental and merely logical. Although Kant tries to show their validity through the help of his transcendental deduction, he ultimately, although implicitly, seems to accept that the a priori resides in the specific constitution of human mind.[21]

If by a priori we mean the presence of certain active, mind-dependent elements in us which organize and synthesize the manifold of representations, there is no point in denying the presence of such an a priori in the philosophy of Hume. Quite similar to the concepts of understanding (Kant), Hume calls his principles "propensities of human nature".

Inspite of great similarity between Hume's principles and Kant's categories there are differences which cannot be overlooked. The Kantian a priori is of a rational and logical character, at least, Kant claims to have discovered them through his transcendental method. The job of Kant's transcendental method is to expose the a priori elements which constitute knowledge. The sense of a priori in the philosophy of Hume is related more to the non-rational (i.e. natural) propensities of our mind.

Hume too maintains that the mental principles are necessary, but the necessity he talks of is not logical necessity. In opposition to the transcendental-logical necessity of Kant, Hume's sense of necessity is the original certainty of our belief. Quite parallel to Kant's transcendental method, there is the experimental method of reasoning in Hume.

The a priori of Kant, to use an expression of Dilthey's, is "rigid and dead" (starr und tot). The Humean a priori, on the other hand, is more flexible and nearer to the course of our evolutionary experience.

In opposition to the categories of understanding, Hume's principles represent the very ways in which our human nature works. Even Kant's

---

[21] Cf. Chapter VI here, "Towards a Theory of 'Anthropocentrism' with regard to Naturalism and Criticism."

categories can be said to rest ultimately on the very constitution of our mind. And it is just a surd fact that our mind works in this and in no other way. Unlike the categories, the principles are not the formal functions of our pure reason but rather the operations of our human nature. The problem of validation and justification presents a challenge not only to Kant but also to Hume. But Kant, unlike Hume, tries to give a transcendental deduction which really is the very sense of validation and justification. Hume on the other hand tries to show their practical necessity in all our enquiries.

Much of the programmatic and architectonic similarities between Hume and Kant, as we have tried to show, result from their quite similar theory of imagination. We have already shown the place of and the role played by imagination in the philosophy of Hume and Kant, respectively, while discussing the problem of sense and understanding. Here we propose to show in what way the concept of imagination is related to the principles as well as to the categories.

The Humean theory of imagination has failed to attract the attention of the commentators on Hume until recently. Our discussion in Chapter II has made clear that it is not fully out of place if we speak of an "a priori imagination" also in the philosophy of Hume. The universal, regular and unchangeable qualities of our imagination determine the nature of all those principles which are essential for the constitution of our knowledge and experience. Thus, the Humean and Kantian imagination is the reservoir of all unitary principles. It works so deeply in our soul that we are rarely conscious that it is there. It is thus imagination and not reason that is the most active center of our mind.

We have already shown that Hume and Kant are badly in need of a third factor which might play the role of a mediator between the sense and reason. Imagination is this third component. According to Kant, it is a blind but indispensible function of our soul. Hume goes so far as to identify imagination with human nature and to say that in the absence of the universal qualities of our imagination "human nature must immediately perish and go to ruin."[22]

Imagination is the very seat of all unification. The most original unity is the unity of transcendental apperception. Kant's concept of productive imagination is a synthesizing faculty; it brings unity into the chaotic manifold of representations. And this unity is ultimately grounded in our ability to conceive that "I think" must accompany

[22] D. Hume: *Treatise*, p. 225.

all our representations. Kant repudiates the merely psychological and empirical treatment of imagination, for such a treatment fails to do justice to another very important side of it. Imagination fulfils not only a psychological function, it is also capable of transcendental activity. It is this transcendental imagination which is the pivotal and most original faculty in all critical philosophy.

To the most radical question "why should and must there be such a faculty as imagination?", Kant's answer is: first, because the de facto existence of experience needs such a principle and, second, because the results of the transcendental deduction legitimize the introduction of the faculty of imagination. But the real answer can be derived from Kant's theory of "schematism". And imagination, according to this theory, is a creative faculty in the depth of the human soul.[23]

There is a great unanimity among philosophers regarding the nature and function of imagination in the philosophy of Kant. But views widely differ regarding the nature and function of Humean imagination. And Hume himself is at least partly to blame because of the vagueness of his theory of imagination. The following extracts from Hume's "Treatise" put his theory of imagination before us:

"But it may be objected, that the imagination, according to my own confession, being the ultimate judge of all systems of philosophy, I am unjust in blaming the ancient philosophers for making use of that faculty, and allowing themselves to be entirely guided by it in their reasonings. In order to justify myself, I must distinguish in the imagination betwixt the principles which are *permanent, irresistable*, and *universal*; such as the customary transition from causes to effects, and from effects to causes: And the principles, which are changeable, weak, and irregular; ... The former are the foundation of all our thoughts and actions, so that upon their removal human nature must immediately perish and go to ruin. The latter are neither unavoidable to mankind nor necessary, or so much as useful in the conduct of life; but on the contrary are observ'd only to take place in weak minds, and being opposite to the other principles of custom and reasoning, may easily be subverted by a due contrast and opposition. For this reason the former are received by philosophy, and the latter rejected ..." (my italics).[24]

Imagination is the power to transpose and change our ideas in such a way that they are enlivened with the immediacy and vivacity of our

<hr>

[23] Cf. I. Kant: *Kritik der reinen Vernunft*, A 78.
[24] D. Hume: *Treatise*, p. 225.

impressions. But these impressions are no longer the impressions of sensations but are impressions of reflection. The most general activities of our thought are all due to imagination. Hume identifies the human nature with the most general and established properties of the imagination.[25]

After his devastating criticism of sensualistic as well as rationalistic tradition, Hume must find a "way out" which enables him to regain the lost world.

In his criticism of Cartesian doubt, Hume, very much in the spirit of Husserlian phenomenology, maintains that once the world is put to question, we shall be completely at a loss to prove its existence. He speaks in this context humbly of his "sceptical solution". In this solution he brings in the imagination to solve the problem of transcendence which is essential not only to epistemology but also to moral philosophy.

Imagination is generally equated with our fancy which is the faculty to produce fictions. And when Hume charges the ancient philosophers in his "Treatise", he of course takes imagination in this, so to say, "weak" sense of the term "imagination". It is this imagination that must have led the ancient philosophers to produce the fictions such as substance, soul and so on. Hume's own view of imagination equates it with some universal faculty in us having the quality of vivacity. "Without this quality", Hume clearly points out, "by which *the mind* enlivens some ideas beyond others, we could never assent to any argument, *nor carry our view beyond those few objects*, which are present to our senses ... The memory, senses and understanding are, therefore, all of them founded on the imagination" (my italics).[26]

Since imagination possesses the qualities which are permanent, irresistable and universal, Hume invokes to it in order to substantiate an "operation of our mind" which he terms "belief" and which is the real source of our conviction that there is an external world.

After fixing the non-fictional character of his imagination, Hume asks: "Wherein, therefore, consists the difference between fiction and belief?" And he answers: "The distinction between fiction and belief lies in some sentiment or feeling which is attached to the latter and not to the former."[27] Thanks to the vivacity-character of our imagination, we "believe" in the existence of the external world and other objects

25 Cf. *ibid.*, p. 267.
26 D. Hume: *Treatise*, p. 265.
27 D. Hume: *Enquiries*, pp. 17 ff

which we "conceive" in a completely different way than the objects of fictions. It is the "how" of conception and not the "what" of conception that makes the difference.

Since Descartes, the problem of the unity of consciousness has been a constant theme of modern philosophy. And Hume and Kant contribute towards the solution of this problem in their own ways. They are in search of an idea of unity which is vivid, clear and certain. Although Kant uses the transcendental apperception, the "I think" which accompanies all our representations, still his use of it aims at different results than Descartes' did. The "I think" of Kant is such that it can be attached to each and every one of our mental contents. Nothing can be understood as a unity unless it has a stamp of transcendental unity on it.

It is beyond doubt that Kant's treatment of the problem of unity means a great advance over Hume, who first tried to show that the problem of unity is a matter of association of our ideas. But both of them failed to find a satisfactory theory of self which could reconcile all the different "selves" we talk of. The point of departure for them both is the same vague idea of our self.

Hume compares the soul "to a republic of commonwealth, in which the several members are united by the reciprocal ties of government and subordination, and give rise to other persons, who propagate the same republic in the incessant changes of it's parts. And as the same individual republic may not only change its members but also its laws and constitution, in like manner the same person may vary his character and disposition, as well as his impressions and ideas, *without losing his identity*" (my italics).[28]

Hume clearly differentiates here between "sameness" and "identity" although he fails to work out this point even to his own satisfaction. But he seems to be sure that whenever we talk of an identical something "our mind passes easily from the idea of ourselves to that of any other object related to us."[29] What is this if not a counterpart to the Kantian "I think" which accompanies all our representations (perceptions)!

Quite similar to the transcendental imagination of Kant which gives unity to our experience, the imagination of Hume serves a similar purpose of unifying and organizing our experience.

Kant is fully in agreement with Hume about the universality of the

[28] D. Hume: *Treatise*: p. 261.
[29] *Ibid.*, p. 340.

causal principle. This principle cannot be deduced from experience, for experience presupposes it. But since Kant starts from the traditional formal (Aristotelean) logic and takes it to be a complete one, he is led to list the functions of our understanding. His metaphysical deduction, as we shall see, utilizes this *formal* clue to fix the number of the categories. And this means that the transition from formal logic to transcendental logic is complete in Kant's philosophy. That no such transition can be made has been shown by many distinguished Kantian scholars.[30] Since Hume was very sceptical towards all formalizations, he did not try any such transition.

Whereas Kant solves the problem of causality by making it a transcendental category, Hume, a non-transcendentalist by temperament, tries to link the synthetic and yet universal character of causality with his theory of imagination, and the universal causal transition gets the stamp of a universal transition via imagination.

Both Hume and Kant are proposing a solution to the problem of the objective validity of the principles as well as categories. The point of departure for both of them is that the necessity we are in search of lies not in the objects but in the subject. But whereas Kant follows the transcendental course, Hume takes the "natural" course in order to analyse the subjective contribution of human mind.

The Humean solution starts from the human nature, human constitution, and tries to show that it is the real seat of all the principles which guide, explain and justify our knowledge. The Kantian solution, on the other hand, takes human reason as the very seat of all the categories. Reason for Kant is a pure faculty endowed with a priori principles. Hume's theory of the principles is not dependent on a particular theory of formal logic.

Hume, and not Kant, was very sceptical regarding the so-called synthetic a priori judgments. Hume would never favor a solution of this problem on the Kantian line. This means that a "naturalistic" interpretation of the Humean principles is the only possible way to explain and understand his theory of the principles. Kant's theory, conversely remains more or less within the framework of rationalism although it is not the rationalism of the dogmatic type.

The transcendental categories of Kant are more formal and rational, whereas the principles of Hume are of non-rational and natural character. It was Hume's firm conviction that no logic which corresponds to the field of the relations of ideas could throw light on the problems

---

[30] Cf. Walsh: *Reason and Experience*, p. 168.

within the field of matters of fact. Kant, on the other hand, thought that by connecting the categories with the judgments, we could solve the problem of the validity of the categories.

Hume's principles are "natural" and this means that they are not irrational. They are not irrational because they are the principles suitable to our experience. The operations of nature are independent of our thought and reasoning and the term "natural" stands for the manner our nature shows in its relation to whatever we come in contact with. The most natural is the most agreeable.

Hume disputes the very possibility of any demonstration of the principles (categories), for that would really mean banishing the principles from the field of matters of fact and existence to the field of the relations of ideas. And this would in turn imply that the principles are not of synthetic character. But this does not mean that Hume makes these principles to be merely empirical. They are natural and that means that they are independent of our reason and experience. Thus, Hume's theory of the apriori aims at working out some type of ,,natural a priori". Programmatically, the Kantian term "transcendental" seems to correspond to the Humean term "natural".

There is an unmistakable sign characterizing our modern researches. This sign consists of the conviction in the modern man, motivated by the recent developments mainly in the science of biology, that the best key towards the solution of philosophical problems lies in naturalistic interpretation. This may be one of the reasons for revival of the interest in Hume. Since natural is opposed to artificial and intellectual, any attempt to derive the principles (categories) intellectually-formally would imply some sort of artificiality. Kant hoped far too much from the mediation of formal logic which, he thought, would bridge the gap between logic and the categories in the field of knowledge. The most foundational basis is human nature and its constitution. And Kant's criticism may itself be said to be based on the special constitution of man's mind. This means that there is sense in making Hume's "naturalism" more critical and Kant's "criticism" more natural. We shall come to discuss this problem in the last chapter of this book.

Although Hume never discussed the problem of deduction the way Kant tackled it, still his philosophy seems to contain the idea of a deduction.[31] This means that Hume shows, first, that the principles do not originate in the sense, second, they are also not grounded in reason

---

[31] The term "deduction" is used here in a wider sense and stands for any attempt to show the origin of principles as well as of categories.

and, third, that they represent the different "propensities" of our mental constitution. It is thus clear that Hume denies the possibility of either a purely formal-logical (rational) or a sensualistically empirical deduction. Kant is very much in agreement on this point with Hume.

It is interesting to note that Hume and Kant are convinced of having worked out and presented to the world a "new science". They are further convinced that hardly anyone before them thought of such a foundational science which, being very fundamental, would revolutionize philosophical thinking.[32]

Kant in his "Prolegomena" remembers Hume and particularly the latter's "hint" (Wink) which, as we shall presently see, means Hume's devasting criticism of the very causal principle. This is the famous question in the "Treatise": Why a cause is always necessary? Hume does not ask whether a cause is necessary. This is a point he never puts to question. Thus, it is really the deduction that is Hume's problem. And we know that Kant too was anxious to show the origin of the causal principle.

Kant, while remembering Hume, says further in a metaphorical language that Hume failed to rescue his ship (of philosophy) from the deep sea of scepticism. The proud and difficult task Kant is called to master is to pilot the ship. A good and well-versed pilot is necessary if the tedious job of sailing is to be carried out sucessfully. For this purpose, Kant works out a map which codifies the necessary rules and laws of the art of navigation.[33] This is very similar to the Humean anatomy of the human mind.

Kant's very sympathetic consideration of Hume's philosophy is marred by his partial and second-hand knowledge of this philosophy. Consequently, Kant assigns to Hume views which the latter never doubted. Thus, Kant takes for granted that Hume stops short of any constructive suggestion to his otherwise very well oriented criticism of the causal principle.

But the principles of Hume, as we have already seen, can be deduced neither empirically nor rationally nor logically. Kant completely agrees with Hume thus far. But Kant mistook Hume to have undertaken the impossible task of an empirical deduction of the principles (categories). Yet Hume in his "critique of experience" tells us very clearly that experience itself is not the sole ground for the conclusions from experience.

---

[32] Cf. D. Hume. *Treatise*, Introduction; I. Kant: *Kritik der reinen Vernunft*, Preface; *Prolegomena*, Preface.

[33] Cf. I. Kant: *Prolegomena*, Sections 7 and 8.

Hume is in search of the foundation of all conclusions from experience, and his principles are what we may term to be the searched-for foundation.[34]

Hume disputes the very possibility of a rational deduction of the categories and calls such a deduction "fallacious". In Section V Part II of his first "Enquiry", Hume unmistakably presents his own hypothesis: "This operation of the mind, by which we infer like effects from like causes, and "vice-versa", is so essential to the subsistence of all human creatures, it is not probable, that it could be trusted to *the fallacious deduction* of our reason" (my italics).[35]

Provided we agree that there is a sense in speaking of a deduction in the philosophy of David Hume, we may venture to show that corresponding to the "metaphysical deduction" of Kant there is a "natural deduction" in the philosophy of Hume. By "natural" we mean that which is neither empirical nor rational. Natural in the Humean sense is all that is easy and genuine. Natural is opposite to unusual, miraculous and artificial.

Let us take the example of the causal principle in order to show in what way it is natural. Hume maintains that the causal relation contains not only the ideas of "contiguity", "priority" and "constant conjunction" which can easily be shown to hold true on the ground of the association of our ideas, but it also contains – and this is more important – the factor of "necessity", the causal necessity. It is this necessity which is the crux of the problem. Hume tries to trace back this necessity to a certain "feeling", "sentiment" or "manner of conceiving" which is peculiar to our mental constitution. Conclusions from experience are not based on understanding but on some other principle which has more weight and authority. After experience has shown us the customary connections, there arises, Hume says, an operation of the soul which is unavoidable. In the absence of such an operation no "inference" is possible. And "experimental reasoning" depends on a species of instinct or mechanical power that acts in us unknown to ourselves. Thus the real seat of the causal necessity is a propensity of mind which is aroused when sensations and perceptions supply us with the materials of experience.

Hume of course admits that there is no way to justify or prove such a principle or propensity. All that he claims to have shown is, first, that there is such a thing which is more than "mere" association and,

---

[34] Cf. D. Hume: *Enquiries*, p. 30.
[35] D. Hume: *Enquiries*, p. 55.

second, that it is produced neither empirically nor rationally, but rather in a "natural", i.e. easy, manner.

The central thesis of Hume with regard to the theory of the principles of human nature is that the different principles are the different operations of the human mind. They are within us although they need sensations and perceptions so that they may be operative and may constitute our knowledge. Hume compares them with a species of natural instinct, "which no reasoning or process of the thought and understanding is able either to produce or to prevent."[36]

The central doctrine of the "Transcendental Analytic" is the "Transcendental Deduction" of the categories. It is not so much the metaphysical deduction but rather the transcendental deduction which claims to have solved the challenge of Hume. For Hume could be refuted only by successfully showing the validity of the categories without taking the help of a formal logic or of an empirical thinking. This means that there is hardly a satisfactory answer to Hume within the framework of eighteenth century rationalism or empiricism.

Kant had already learned from Hume the barrenness of an empirical or a rational-logical deduction. Kant, while commenting on the philosophy of Locke, praises Hume for having detected the mistakes within the problem of the "whereabouts" of the principles. But Kant further comments that, since Hume failed to see that the categories themselves might be the presupposition for the very possibility of our experience, he explained them with the help of the principle of habit and custom.[37]

The technical name Kant gives to his deduction in this part of his "Critique of Pure Reason" is "transcendental deduction". The central principle of the transcendental deduction is that it is and must be recognized as the a priori condition for the very possibility of knowledge. Categories are the concepts a priori and their objective validity must be a guaranteed fact because it is they that constitute and make experience possible. Without the mediation of the categories no object of experience can be thought.[38]

The central task of the transcendental deduction is thus to show the

---

[36] *Ibid.*, p. 47.

[37] "Der berühmte Locke hatte, aus Ermangelung dieser Betrachtung, und weil er reine Begriffe des Verstandes in der Erfahrung antraf, sie auch von der Erfahrung abgeleitet, und verfuhr doch so inkonsequent, daß er damit Versuche zu Erkenntnissen wagte, die weit über die Erfahrungsgrenze hinausgehen. David Hume erkannte, um das letztere tun zu können, sei es notwendig, daß diese Begriffe ihren Ursprung a priori haben müßten ..." (I. Kant: *Kritik der reinen Vernunft*, B. 127).

[38] *Ibid.*, A 94: B 126.

objective validity of the concepts. The whole complex of the deduction argument has two external determinants: The considerations of Herz center round the difficulties and inadequacies of the "Dissertation"-doctrine of Kant. This was also the main content of Kant's famous letter to Herz. The second determinant is Hume's "critique of a priori knowledge". Hume has clearly demonstrated the inadequacy of a priori consideration with regard to the problem of causality. If we consider things a priori, anything may be said to be the cause of anything else.[39]

Although Kant first confines his discussion to the problem of causality, he very well knows that Hume's criticism of causality applies to all the twelve categories. And Kant in fact does extend the field of application. This further aggravates his fear with regard to the sceptical consequences of Hume's philosophy.

To meet the challenge of Hume, which spreads like wildfire, Kant develops his deduction argument through different stages. Hume's attacks on the causal maxim convinced Kant that it is logically indemonstrable.[40] In Kant's language, there is no *quid juris* question about the causal maxim. All that can be done is to answer it *quid facti*. And it is this *quid facti* answer which shows that the real seat of the necessary connection is not association but a certain propensity (natural belief) of our mind. And belief is a certain impression which no understanding can produce.

Kant is bent upon showing that the causal maxim is a necessary truth in the sense of the category despite the fact that it is neither a mere association nor a logical truth. In other words, he wants to prove the synthetic a priori character of this category.

First Kant deals with the question whether there is unsynthesized manifold, i.e. whether perceptions could enter our consciousness even if they do not conform to the concepts. And he really seems to give a positive reply here.[41] Thus, Kant's answer to Hume demands that perceptions must conform to the concepts. This means further that unsynthesized manifold is an impossibility. Hume too accepts the impossibility of unsynthesized manifold. Yet Hume is very sceptical about any deduction of the categories.

Kant substantiates his position: if only empirical concepts are allow-

---

[39] Cf. D. Hume: *Enquiries*, pp. 164–65.

[40] Hume's argument depends mainly on the principle "what is conceivable is possible." Since we can well conceive the contrary of the proposition "every event must have a cause," we must admit the logical indemonstrability of the causal maxim.

[41] Cf. I. Kant: *Kritik der reinen Vernunft*, A 94 95.

ed to produce the badly needed *unity of synthesis*, it must be accidental.[42] And any empirical foundation of a priori would mean that a priori is no longer universal and necessary. The empirical concepts must thus be based on a transcendental ground of unity. Thoughtless intuitions are like undigested food, for they never amount to knowledge (health). To be conscious means to be conscious of something and this *something* always bears the stamp of that original unity which makes all other unifications possible. Finally, Kant differentiates between the subjective association and the real, objective, necessary connection. He is convinced he met the challenge of Hume by making such a distinction between associative subjective and necessary objective connection which is ultimately traced back to the transcendental unity of consciousness (transcendental, original apperception). Kant is further confirmed in his view by his special reading and understanding of Hume; according to Kant, Hume stops short of merely associative connection.

We know that Hume's challenge has two levels and any defender of causal inference has to meet this challenge at both the levels: a) Can we prove that every event must have a cause (the causal maxim) and b) can we necessarily show that future can be inferred from the past. To Kant goes the credit of having successfully met the challenge of Hume at the b) level by showing that all the representations are bound together by universal connection according to *rules*. In other words, if we want to have knowledge we must start with the application of mental apparatus which is there.

In order to meet Hume's other challenge, Kant now maintains that all appearances stand in connection according to *laws*. Here Kant seems to take recourse to the very category without clearly showing the distinction between *mere* association according to rules and real connection according to laws. Hume's own answer is: since the "necessity of connection" is more than *mere* association, it must be a *felt* necessity, an oblique operation of our mind in the sense of some *original* principle (propensity) of our human constitution. It follows from what has been said that neither Hume nor Kant succeeded in proving that every event must have a cause. Still the difference between Hume and Kant is that Kant claims to have proved the causal maxim, Hume does not.

The following points seem to follow from what has been said so far:

1. The philosophy of Hume contains a "theory of the principles" programmatically quite similar to that of "the categories". But

---

42 *Ibid.*, A 111.

Hume lags far behind Kant in regard to the systematic working out of his theoretically very good insights.

2. Thus, we can talk of a "theory of mental activity" not only in Kant's philosophy, but also in Hume's.

3. In a certain sense, the principles as well as the categories represent the guides to our experience and knowledge.

4. In the case of Hume, his principles as propensities originate in human nature; the seat of Kantian categories is the human understanding.

5. Neither Hume nor Kant favor a logical deduction of the principles (categories). They are also against an empirical deduction.

6. Inspite of these negative similarities between Hume and Kant with regard to the problem of deduction, Hume's deduction is not a "transcendental", but rather a "natural" one.

7. Unlike Hume, Kant goes even so far as to fix the number of the categories.

8. Kant is convinced that there is no naturalistic-nativistic explanation of the categories; the categories can never be said to have "originated" in the course of the development of human mind because they are given to us a priori. Hume on the other hand speaks of the "generation" of the principles of human nature. Reason itself is a principle of generation in the philosophy of Hume and must be distinguished from the reason in the field of the relations of ideas. The Kantian reason is a fixed faculty endowed with fixed principles.[43]

9. For both Hume and Kant the phenomenon of experience contains active as well as passive elements.

10. There is similarity between their theories of imagination. But in opposition to Kant's transcendental imagination, Hume's imagination may be termed natural.

11. We have already shown that there is a very pregnant sense in speaking of a priori also in the philosophy of David Hume.

12. Neither the principles nor the categories are ultimately demonstrable truths.

13. We cannot ask whether there are principles because that is a point we must start with. The only question that can be asked is how they are and what they are. Kant and Hume seem to differ in their approaches to this latter question.

---

[43] Cf. R. A. Mall, *Experience and Reason*, Chapter X, "Reason."

CHAPTER IV

NATURALISM AND CRITICISM[1]

One of the most interesting and intriguing topics of philosophical debates has been the relation between Hume and Kant. Quite similar to the ontological argument for the existence of God, the Hume-Kant relationship possesses a history of its own.

The central theme of the present chapter is not a review of this history. Rather we undertake to thematize Hume's "naturalism" and Kant's "criticism" as two independent philosophical models towards the solution of the so-called perennial philosophical problems.

In spite of certain architectonic and programmatic similarities, these two philosophical inventories are fundamentally different from each other. And the philosophical intention to reach an agreement at all cost betrays its own dogmatic, if not ideological, tendency.

The naturalism of Hume occupies as central a position in his whole philosophy as the criticism of Kant in his philosophy. Our aim here is to show that Kant's criticism as well as Hume's naturalism may be interpreted in such a way that the former can be made less rigid and the latter less sensualistic. And this would mean a thesis towards a "critical naturalism" as well as "natural criticism".

The following comparative confrontation between Hume's naturalism and Kant's criticism thematizes the problem of the flexibility as well as rigidity of the subordination of the manifold of experience under the original principles of the human mind. It is not so much the fact of relativization to human constitution but rather the "manner" of the same which distinguishes Hume's naturalism from Kant's criticism.

Both Hume's naturalism and Kant's criticism represent two new philosophical attitudes which in their turn aim at revolutionizing the

---

[1] This is an enlarged version and re-edition of my paper "Naturalismus und Kritizismus – Hume and Kant" (contributed to and published in *Akten des 4, Internationalen Kant-Kongresses*, Mainz, Teil II, 1, 1974).

whole field of philosophy. Philosophy must be given a new foundation if she claims the worthy name of a foundational science. Philosophy in this foundational sense is neither a natural science nor simply a discipline within humanities.

Beliefs, i.e. operations of our mind, which are neither due to our reason nor to our senses are nevertheless performances of our nature, of our constitution. And nature is equated with its own operations which are as regular and constant as those of gravitation in the physical world. The very subtitle of Hume's great work "Treatise" – "Being an Attempt to Introduce the Experimental Method of Reasoning into Moral Subjects" – shows clearly that Hume ventures to apply the Newtonian experimental method to the world of mind. But this is only a functional parallelism, for the contents of Hume's works belong mainly to the world of mental and moral philosophy. His science of man which is the science of all sciences is based upon an analysis and understanding of human nature and its operations. And Hume foreshadows Kant's "Copernican revolution", for he, like Kant, lets the world of objects revolve round the human mind.

Before we come to an adequate positive description of Hume's naturalism, let us begin with a negative description of it:

1. The "naturalism" of Hume is not natural or naturalistic in the sense of "naturalizing" the science of man. His "science of man" is not subordinated to the natural sciences. And Hume tells us very clearly in the opening pages of his "Treatise" that "even *Mathematics, Natural philosophy and Natural Religion*"[2] are dependent on the science of human nature." Thus the most important methodological point of departure for Hume is his conviction that all other sciences bear a necessary relation – greater or less – to the most fundamental and foundational science of man.

2. It is also not natural in the sense of naturalizing or atomizing the life of our consciousness. Hume's teaching of impressions cannot be interpreted only in the sense of sensualistic atomism, for even "feelings", "sentiment" and "belief" represent impressions.[3] The propensities which express themselves in and through the different guiding principles of our nature are the original non-sensuous operations of our mind. The gappy and isolated materials of knowledge cannot give birth to knowledge unless they are organized.

3. It is also not natural in the sense that the possibility of knowledge

2 D. Hume: *Treatise*, Introduction.
3 Cf. C. W. Hendel. *Studies in the Philosophy of David Hume* pp. 379 ff.

can be explained with the help of sense-data philosophy. Hume speaks of scepticism with regard to the senses and he criticizes the natural attitude of the vulgar consciousness for it fails to differentiate between the perception and the object perceived.

4. It is natural in the sense that it maintains an all over subordination of the purely empirical, logical, rational etc. under the operations of human nature. In other words, Hume maintains that nature has determined us to judge, breathe and feel and "'Tis not only in poetry and music, we must follow our taste and sentiment, but likewise in philosophy."[4]

Our different beliefs regarding the external world and other objects, our own identity and so on are different dispositions resulting from the activities of our mind. These common beliefs are not fictions, although they are conceived by the mind. The vivacity-character of belief is what differentiates it from fiction.

Hume's naturalism is the result of his criticism of reason on the one hand and of the senses on the other. The so-called scepticism of Hume culminates in his philosophy of naturalism. This culmination represents the process of a progressive over-coming of the philosophical impasse with which Hume was confronted while scrutinizing the limits of our senses as well as of reason. His naturalism is his "new medium of truth", a discovery which he made in his young years. The main problem of philosophy for Hume is to explain the world order, and he is not convinced of the Cartesian argument which brings forward the conception of a necessary being above nature. The self-sufficiency of nature is the very essence of Hume's naturalism. Hume seems to have learned of "Strato's naturalism" through his study of Bayle's "Dictionary". Cicero, who has been a favorite author and an inspiration to Hume, also thematizes the issue of naturalism in his dialogue "On the Nature of the Gods". Therefore Hume belongs to those followers of Aristotle who tend towards naturalism. Thus, like Kant's criticism, Hume's naturalism is the central hypothesis of his philosophy.

Knowledge according to Hume's central philosophical teaching is an accomplishment neither of the senses nor of reason alone but rather of human nature, human imagination. A positive description of Hume's naturalism aims at showing the natural, i.e. easy, genuine character of the different guiding and constituting principles.[5] Since these principles represent the different propensities as well as dispositions of our

<hr>

4 D. Hume: *Treatise*, p. 103.
5 Cf. D. Humo: *Treatise*, Book I, Part IV.

mind they cannot be determined a priori if by a priori we mean the a priori in the field of the relations of ideas. Had they been a priori in nature in this sense, they would have had only an analytic necessity. But their non-intuitive and non-demonstrative character show that they belong to the field of matters of fact. The term "natural" is opposed to the rational, logical and empirical, in one word, to the sceptical. Hume's naturalism is thus a defense of the rights of human nature against the claims of the senses and reason.

The central thesis of Hume's naturalism is his assertion of an absolute and uncontrollable necessity with which nature has determined us to judge as well as to feel. Like Kant's criticism, Hume's naturalism is a systematic inventory with the aim of ascertaining the powers of senses, reason and nature. Hume says that the most important act of belief "is more properly an act of the sensitive than of the cogitative part of our natures."[6] This is his hypothesis of naturalism which he wants to make clear to the reader.

Our human nature possesses its own original ways which we can neither challenge nor afford to deny. They are too powerful when compared to our reflection and the principles of our unsteady imagination. Belief is no simple act of thought without any peculiar manner of conception. It is, as Hume says, "some sensation or peculiar manner of conception, which 'tis impossible for mere ideas and reflections to destroy."[7]

In order to show the non-sensuous as well as non-rational character of the natural principles like custom, habit, belief, imagination etc., Hume states: Were they sensuous in nature they must be given to our senses. But we know that this is not the case. The principle that every event must have a cause cannot be due to sensuous experience. The principle of causality transcends the limits of our senses. Were they rational they must be demonstrable. But this too does not hold true, for the principles of human nature cannot be demonstrated as the truths in the field of the relations of ideas. Thus, the naturalism of Hume is the destruction of both the mighty traditions in philosophy – sensualistic empiricism as well as dogmatic rationalism.[8]

It is too idle a question to ask why nature works in this and only this way rather than in any other way. To ask this is just to ask for what is not the case. The main task of Hume's philosophy of human nature is to discover and formulate its different ways of working. The question

---

[6] D. Hume: *Treatise*, p. 183.
[7] *Ibid.*, p. 184.
[8] Cf. *ibid.*, Book I, Part IV.

of "how" and "why" must not be confounded. Of course, we may conceive of nature working in other ways but who can tell ultimately why in this way and not in some other way. The ultimate reason, if there is any, of why milk is white is unknown to us.[9]

Hume's naturalism is more akin to Husserl's phenomenology than to Kant's intellectualization and transcendentalization of the field of our knowledge and activities. Inspite of the firm conviction of Kant to carry out and fulfil the task left by Hume, the philosophical continuity from Hume onward runs not so much via Kant but via Meinong, Brentano, James, Dilthey and so on to Husserl.[10]

The naturalism of Hume reigns supreme not only in his epistemology but also in his moral and religious philosophy. The most fundamental science Hume conceives of is the "science of man". And more in the spirit of Husserl than that of Kant, Hume maintains that all the sciences, even the natural sciences, are nothing but accomplishments of human nature and its principles.[11] But nevertheless there can be no denial that there is also a great programmatic similarity between Hume's science of human nature and Kant's science of the pure reason. Whereas Kant is busy in furnishing the natural sciences with a philosophical explanation and foundation, Hume is more radical and tries to show the dependence of natural as well as mathematical sciences on that of the human nature.

It is Hume's naturalism that gives a particular turn to his theory of knowledge which is critical of both reason and sense. The character of the necessity peculiar to our judgments in the field of our knowledge belonging to matters of fact is not the analytic, logical and absolute necessity which can be demonstrated. It is a necessity relative to human constitution but it is also a concept of necessity which formally possesses the same structure as the other necessity. The necessity contingent to human nature is not empirical necessity either. Hume does not doubt the proposition "the sun will rise tomorrow in the east". All he wants to maintain is "that our Certainty or the Falsehood of that proposition proceeded neither from Intuition nor Demonstration; but from another source."[12] And this source, this seat of the different principles is human nature, human imagination.

---

[9] Hume's naturalism asks the question "how" rather than "why." In the introduction to his "Treatise," Hume clearly maintains the futility of all abstruse metaphysical questions (Cf. *ibid.*, Introduction).

[10] Cf. R. A. Mall: *Experience and Reason*, Introductory and Chapter VIII.

[11] Cf. *ibid.*, pp. 78 ff.

[12] Greig: *Letters*, p. 185; cf. also Chapter VI here.

Hume's naturalism does away with the primacy of reason over the senses and of the senses over reason. Kant is not a successor to Hume in so far as he favors reason more than the senses, and Husserl is a successor to Hume in so far as he does not favor reason as a fixed faculty endowed with fixed principles. Hume might be said to have favored the senses more than reason but this impression is primarily because Hume failed to develop his hypothesis of naturalism to such an extent as to make all misunderstandings impossible.

Hume never hesitates, even for a moment, to decide in favor of imagination. Imagination, as we have seen, is endowed with universal, regular and permanent qualities which also help characterize human nature, human constitution. Hume's naturalism may thus be termed "imaginative naturalism" in order to differentiate it from other types of naturalism. It is not metaphysical materialism, for Hume is against all speculative metaphysics. His naturalism takes nature to be the very dynamic instance which explains and justifies our behavior in all the fields of our enquiry.

In Book I, Part IV, of his "Treatise", Hume undertakes a critical examination of some philosophical systems – both of ancient and modern philosophy. In his critical discussion of ancient philosophy Hume clearly shows the fictional character of some of the fundamental categories, such as substance, soul etc. The ancient philosophers, when confronted with a phenomenon, consoled themselves by inventing words like faculty and occult quality which they felt would explain the phenomenon.

Before Kant had composed his "Critique of Pure Reason" he feared never being able to present his ideas and discoveries fully and perfectly to the world. The following extract from a long letter written by Hume to a famous Scotch physician points to a quite similar fear of Hume's: "... Every one who is acquainted either with the philosophers or critics, knows that there is nothing yet established in either of these two sciences, and that they contain little more than endless disputes,[13] even in the most fundamental articles. Upon examination of these, I found a certain boldness of temper growing in me, which was not inclined to submit to any authority in these subjects, but led me to seek out some new medium, by which truth might be established ... I have

---

[13] In his preface to the first edition of his "Critique of Pure Reason," Kant speaks of metaphysics as a battlefield of endless disputes ("Der Kampfplatz dieser endlosen Streitigkeiten heißt nun Metaphysik").

collected the rude materials for many volumes; but in reducing these
to words, ... this I found impracticable for me ... Here lay my greatest
calamity. I had no hopes of delivering my opinions with such elegance
and neatness, as to draw to me the attention of the world ..."[14]

The new scene of thought Hume speaks of is that all judgments upon
truth and conduct depend on human nature, and without a knowledge
of human nature there would never be a true understanding of the
things and beings which are the objects of our enquiry. Hume's naturalism is the very rationale of his philosophy.

There is a remarkable tendency in human nature to sympathies and
antipathies. They constitute our unsteady inclinations and trivial propensity of the imagination. Such propensity reigns supreme in children,
poets and ancient philosophers, and it can be checked and suppress-
ed only by our genuine reflection on our human nature. "We must
pardon children", Hume writes rather ironically, "because of their age;
poets because they profess to follow implicitly the suggestions of their
fancy: But what shall we find to justify our philosophers in so single
a weakness?"[15] Thus, Hume's main charge against the ancient
philosophers is that they neglected the study of human nature and
consulted only their fancy in erecting big speculative systems without
any regard to human nature. Such systems are clear and logically very
neat but this neatness is derived at the cost of the barrenness of these
systems.

Hume shows a similar pretention in modern philosophy which to him
lands in an incorrigible dualism, scepticism and solipsism. This is true
of both the main currents of modern philosophy – dogmatic rationalism
and sensualistic empiricism. Hume makes his point clear through his
criticism of the Locke-Berkeley tradition on the one hand and of Car-
tesianism on the other. He thus, long before Kant, strongly disputes
the possibility of a rational metaphysics and theology.[16]

Hume's "Treatise" is not simply a completion of the Locke-Berkeley
tradition; it is also not merely a precursor of Kant's "Critique of Pure
Reason". His naturalism is his own new conception of philosophy and
it discovers the principles of human nature through the assistance of the
non-fictional and permanent qualities of human nature. The naturalism

---

[14] Greig: *Letters*, I, pp. 16–17.

[15] D. Hume: *Treatise*, p. 225.

[16] A first reading of Book I, Part IV of the "Treatise" seems to convince us that Hume
is very sceptical about certain very fundamental issues in philosophy – issues like soul, identity etc. But a careful re-reading fully convinces us that Hume in these passages is strongly
reacting against the teaching of Descartes and the Cartesians.

of Hume is his "descriptive phenomenology "of human nature and its propensities.

In his quest for a sure and certain foundation of human inference, Hume pacifies his impatient critics by clearly pointing out that after the bankruptcy of reason and the senses we must discover some other source which explains and justifies our inferences in the fields of human knowledge and conduct.

We can never ascertain why a cause is always necessary. All we can do is to show that this is how our human nature works and must work if the factual behavior of human beings is to have a basis. The real question thus is not why there is the causal maxim but why we find it necessary to attribute a cause to order of any kind. The following line of argument, which is generally taken by philosophers, begs the very question: everything must have a cause for the simple reason that, if it had not one, it would produce itself or would be produced by nothing. Philosophers like Hobbes, Clarke and Locke argue more or less in the manner just mentioned. Hume very honestly begs the philosopher and the reasoner not to introduce the thing itself or nothing as the cause, when we consider the whole situation under the exclusion of cause. Thus it is a pretention to maintain that the necessary character of cause can be proved and demonstrated; all that these pious attempts at demonstration really do show is that the human nature from its very constitution must act in this way. Thus, we may maintain that Hume's naturalism provides us with a natural explanation of the causal principle.

Human nature is the sole foundation of these principles. They are called natural because: a) they are neither a priori in the analytic sense of the term nor merely empirical in the purely sensualistic sense and b) they are the most original, genuine ways in which our human nature works and guides us. The method Hume uses to discover these principles is the famous method of "experimental reasoning".[17]

Hume's own answer to the question of whether he is a sceptic or not is a classical clue to an understanding of his naturalism. "Shou'd it here be ask'd me ... whether I be really one of those sceptics, who hold all is uncertain, and that our judgment is not in *any* thing possest of *any* measures of truth and falsehood; I shou'd reply, that this question is entirely superfluous, and that neither I, nor any other person was

---

[17] This method of Hume has certain similarities with the phenomenological method of "eidetic variation." The aim of both these methods is a descriptive explanation and not an explanatory description.

ever sincerely and constantly of that opinion ... Whoever has taken the pains to refute the cavils of this *total* scepticism, has really disputed without an antagonist, and endeavour'd by arguments to establish a faculty, which nature has antecedently implanted in the mind, and rendered unavoidable."[18] This passage makes fully clear that Hume is not only a non-sceptic but also a critic of scepticism.

Hume's naturalism is thus his middle path avoiding both the extremes of a transcendentalism which postulates a transcendental "I" and of the vulgar consciousness which identifies the object of perception with the act of perceiving.

The most original and fundamental ground of all syntheses is the human nature in the sense of human imagination which possesses the quality of transcending the gappy data of the senses and making the regular more regular and constant. It is a principle of continuation and prolongation. But human nature, as Hume understands it, is no postulation; it is not a logical synthesis either. It's de facto being there is reason enough that it is there.

There is a unity within the different branches of human knowledge. A similar type of unity is also to be found within the different categories of human behavior. The unity or the uniformity is the constituting principle of human nature, nay it is human nature itself.[19] We have already mentioned the young discovery by Hume. The priority of human nature means its primacy over reason and the senses. This is the hypothesis which made Hume so restless in his twenties, and this is also the hypothesis which lends unity to his philosophy.

The famous discussion of the problem of the external world in Book I, Part IV, Section II of the "Treatise" deals not with the question "whether" but "how" there is a world. This section starts with the declaration of the impotent character of our reason which a sceptic uses in defending his reason. And a reason that reasons against reason can defend nothing. There is a formal similarity of approach between Hume's discussion of the problem of the external world and Kant's discussion of the question regarding the possibility of synthetic a priori judgments. Kant too does not ask whether there must be such judgments, but he shows only how they are possible. That they are there is conveyed to him by his study of the natural as well as mathematical sciences. But Hume is more radical than Kant who, as Husserl has

---

[18] D. Hume: *Treatise*, p. 183.
[19] Cf. Schaefer: *David Hume*, p. 160.

very clearly pointed out, skips over the problem of the world (Lebenswelt).

We may well term Hume's naturalism "descriptive" because, very much in the spirit of a descriptive phenomenologist, Hume subordinates the question "why" and "what" to the question "how". Since the question "why" cannot be ultimately answered it is futile to ask it. "My general conclusion will be", N. K. Smith writes," that the establishment of a purely naturalistic conception of human nature by the thorough subordination of reason to feeling and instinct is the determining factor in Hume's philosophy."[20]

There is nothing more ambiguous than the term "nature". But Hume clarifies his meaning when he describes and defines nature by its characters of uniformity, regularity and constancy. Hume nowhere in his philosophical literature discusses the problem of a) nature at large and b) nature just as human nature.[21] Even if we accept that our human nature is in some sense a part of the nature at large we cannot explain this nature at large without the help of the very principles of human nature. And this is the main claim of Hume's naturalism.

Starting from his theory of knowledge and proceeding to his philosophy of religion it is the self-same naturalism which works in and unites the different parts of his philosophy. And this is one of the main features of the architectonic and programmatic similarity between Hume's naturalism and Kant's criticism.

Like Hume, Kant also claims to have revolutionized the field of philosophy. And Kant announced this revolution with his "Inaugural Dissertation" of 1770. But he developed his critical philosophy in his "Critique of Pure Reason" in 1781. This new tool of "criticism" helped Kant to banish rational psychology as well as theology from the field of a scientific philosophy. Kant also established a novel theory of knowledge and banished metaphysics. In all these achievements, he is far superior to Hume who insisted rather too much on his distinction between relations of ideas and matters of fact. Hume failed to develop a theory of judgment which could serve as the basis of finding the table of categories. Hume's view of logic is too narrow to be able to show him a way in the field of matters of fact.

Kant's critical philosophy is a systematic discovery (inventory) of the powers and propensities of the human mind. Very much in the

---

[20] N. K. Smith: *Mind*, 1905.
[21] Cf. R. A. Mall: *Hume's Concept of Man*, pp. 107 ff.

spirit of Hume, Kant too undertakes the task of scrutinizing out subjective contributions to knowledge. And philosophy is in fact the "critique" of this contribution. It is true that the main outcome of Kant's
"Critique of Pure Reason" consists of the discovery of the limits of
this reason, and such a limitation in turn means that human reason as
such must not cross its boundary lines. But the most positive result
of all this is that Kant makes room for faith and that means that there
is a practical reason which saves us from disparaging consequences.
Thus, the mission of Kant's critical philosophy is twofold.

Hume and Kant both accept that there are mind-dependent elements
in our experience, but Kant unlike Hume terms these elements "a
priori" and claims to have presented the world not only with a "table
of categories" but also with a "list of the categories". Kant's critical
philosophy, as he views it, contains or is, historically speaking, not only
an answer to Hume but also to Descartes and Leibniz.

What is the most salient feature of Kant's criticism? How are we
to understand this middle path between rationalism and empiricism?
In what way does it do justice to both rational and empirical traditions?
To what extent has Kant succeeded in justifying his claim of having
given an absolute foundation to all experience -- actual as well as possible? More to Kant than to Hume belongs the credit of showing that
if we have knowledge, as we certainly have, the senses and the intellect
must meet. This meeting ground is prepared by his critical inventory.
Besides his solitary contribution to the field of moral philosophy,
Kant's contribution to the field of theory of knowledge is what en-
titles him to be called one of the great philosophical geniuses in the
tradition of European philosophy. The genius of Kant blends together
in a harmonious novelty the different influences of Wolf, Descartes,
Leibniz, Hume, Rousseau, Newton, etc.

In his "Prolegomena", Kant describes his "Critique of Pure Reason"
as the real "Mittelweg zwischen dem Dogmatismus und dem Skeptizismus".[22] He clarifies his position when he credits Hume with having
rightly attacked the dogmatic rationalism but takes him to task for
having introduced scepticism in philosophy. Kant carries this reading
and understanding of Hume throughout his philosophy. Kant undoubtedly accepts the hint (Wink) given by Hume, but he deplores Hume
for having fallen short of founding the new science of which nobody
ever conceived. The critical philosophy of Kant, as he himself says, is

---

[22] I. Kant: *Prolegomena*, Section 58.

determined according to "principles" (Prinzipien) which are sure and certain.[23]

Kant's criticism is his new inventory and his critical method is essentially a method of reflection on the "scientific experience".[24] The human intellect as the unity of logical functions is the very object of the critical philosophy.

Before we go further in our critical and comparative discussion of Kant's criticism and Hume's naturalism, it is necessary to understand in what sense Kant uses the two very important terms "dogmatic" and "sceptical". The term "dogmatic" is used in two quite different senses in his critical philosophy: in a negative and a positive sense.

In opposition to the historical knowledge which is a posteriori and individual, "dogmatic" is used in the sense of the general, rational a priori knowledge. The positive sense of the term "dogmatic" is the knowledge which is evident because it is based on reason. It is this latter sense that is accepted by Kant.

The term "sceptical" also possesses a positive as well as a negative sense. In its first use, which Kant favors, "sceptical" stands for a method, a procedure, a way. This means in our practice not to assert anything unless all the arguments for and against it have been taken into account. Every assertion requires a critical-sceptical pre-examination. Scepticism in this sense is recommended and is of great help to us. In its negative sense, it stands for a position which doubts everything and denies the very possibility of knowledge. This sense of scepticism goes hand in hand with the negative sense of dogmatism.

Kant thus makes a distinction between scepticism as a philosophy and as a method. Since Kant takes Hume to have introduced scepticism in philosophy, he undertakes the task of refuting him. Had Kant studied Hume thoroughly, he would have easily realized that Hume too is a critic of scepticism. The difference between them lies rather in the manner of how they refute scepticism.

Unless we accept these two senses of the term "sceptical", we can

---

[23] "Allein diese Prolegomena werden ihn dahin bringen einzusehen, daß es eine ganz neue Wissenschaft sei, von welcher niemand auch nur den Gedanken vorher gefaßt hatte, wovon selbst die bloße Idee unbekannt war, und wozu von allem bisher Gegebenen nichts genutzt werden konnte als allein der Wink, den Humes Zweifel geben konnten, der gleichfalls nichts von einer dergleichen möglichen förmlichen Wissenschaft ahnte, sondern sein Schiff, um es in Sicherheit zu bringen, auf den Strand (den Skeptizismus) setzte ..." (*Ibid.* Preface).

[24] Herein lies one of the most fundamental differences between Hume's and Kant's theories of experience. Unlike Kant, Hume does not restrict his analysis to only the "scientific experience" but to experience in general. Neither reason nor experience is a fixed entity for Hume and this means that the philosophical continuity from Hume to Husserl is not via Kant but through Meinong, Brentano, James, Avenarius, Mach and Dilthey.

hardly understand Kant's insistence that the proofs of the fourfold antinomies are no delusion (Blendwerke). The transcendental dialectic does not favor a sceptical philosophy but only furthers the cause of a sceptical method which is of much use.[25] Thus there is a sense in maintaining that Kant's critical philosophy is not completely against scepticism. Very much in the spirit of Berkeley, Kant is convinced he has banished scepticism from philosophy for all time. We know the actual answer of Hume to the claims of Berkeley who, in the eyes of Hume, is regarded as the father of modern scepticism, but it is left to our imagination to guess Hume's answer to Kant.

We have already shown the very important role played by the faculty of imagination in the philosophy of Kant as well as in that of Hume. Imagination, Kant maintains, is an art concealed in the depths of the human soul. It is, in opposition to the understanding, not only creative but also more comprehensive. The synthesis of the manifold in imagination bears the name "transcendental" which is the most original unity (transcendental apperception) necessarily presupposed by all other forms of unities. The Kantian theory of critical reflection does not in fact bring this unity into being, it rather presupposes it and shows its necessary character. Thus, the critical philosophy of Kant is an attempt to analyze our human constitution and its ways of working.

The criticism of Kant is bent upon bringing about a cooperation between the rational and the sensuous, the senses and the intellect. Neither the senses nor the intellect should lose their peculiar character, for an intellectualization of the senses would lead to dogmatic rationalism and a sensualization of the intellect to dogmatic sensualism. Inspite of all these precautions, Kant's criticism is not fully free from a certain subordination of the sensuous under the non-sensuous, empirical under the non-empirical. A similar criticism may also be levied against Hume's naturalism which tends to subordinate reason under the senses. If it is true to say that Kant could not fully get rid of his "rationalistic heritage",[26] so it is not less true to maintain that Hume, too, failed to overcome his "sensualistically empirical heritage".

---

[25] In his "Kritik der reinen Vernunft," Kant writes: "Die transzendentale Dialektik tut also keineswegs dem Skeptizismus einigen Vorschub, wohl aber der skeptischen Methode, welche an ihr ein Beispiel ihres großen Nutzens aufweisen kann, wenn man die Argumente der Vernunft in ihrer größten Freiheit gegeneinander auftreten läßt, die, ob sie gleich zuletzt nicht dasjenige, was man suchte, dennoch jederzeit etwas Nützliches und zur Berichtigung unserer Urteile Dienliches, liefern werden" (A 507; B 535).

[26] Kibéd explains Kant's subordination of the sensuous under the non-sensuous in the following way: "Daß Kant bei der Forderung der Zuordnung und Unterordnung der zwei verschiedenen Seinsbereiche nicht an die andere Möglichkeit, nämlich an die Unterordnung

One of the most salient features of Kant's critical philosophy is the central demand to subordinate the sensuous manifold under the concepts of the understanding. Since the categories possess a permanent and unchangeable validity, Kant did not take the other possibility of subordinating the intellect under the senses.

Kant is very clear on the point regarding the *manner* of the determination of the sensuous through the non-sensuous. He maintains this manner to be ultimately inexplicable (unerklärlich).[27] Even if we leave this inexplicable character of the determination aside, which undoubtedly is very similar to Hume's still clearer pronouncements regarding the futility and barrenness of our asking for the ultimate principles of human nature, we still may discover some similarity between Hume's naturalism and Kant's criticism.

Both Hume and Kant are convinced that neither the senses nor the intellect, if left to themselves, can give rise to knowledge. The sensuous manifold must be "spelled out" by the concepts of our understanding. But the real character of this very certainty, lying behind this conviction common to both Hume and Kant, is very near to, if not quite similar to, Hume's "natural belief" which is characterized by immediacy, vivacity and liveliness. Of course, Kant tries to account for his conviction by pointing to the reputed and successful sciences like mathematics and physics. But Hume seems to be more radical than Kant on this point, and his science of human nature, quite similar to Husserl's science of the transcendental subjectivity interprets even the sciences like physics and mathematics as the performances of human nature.

Provided Kant is ready to accept that there is hardly any rational-logical guarantee for his conviction regarding the subordination of the sensuous under the non-sensuous for all time to come, except the more or less dogmatic (i.e. not radical enough) recourse to the authorities of the sciences like physics and mathematics, we may well maintain that his critical philosophy, very much in the spirit of Hume's natural philosophy, is based ultimately upon the special constitution of our mind. And such a foundation is neither logical, nor rational; it is also not transcendental. It is a factual foundation pure and simple.

der Kategorien unter die Sinnlichkeit denken konnte, hängt damit zusammen, daß er an der unveränderlichen Geltung der kategorialen Gesetze, welche letztere die Möglichkeit der Mathematik und der Physik erklären und begründen sollten, festhielt und deshalb ihre Geltung durch die Unterordnung der Kategorien unter die Sinnlichkeit nicht gefährden wollte" (*Macht und Ohnmacht der Vernunft*, p. 28).

[27] The ultimate ways of our human nature, of our reason cannot be rationally or logically explained. All that we can do is to show their presence. To ask why they are there is to ask "too much," for the very fact of their being there is enough to satisfy our curiosity.

Kant is certain not only about the actual subordination which really takes place, but he goes further and maintains that it will always be the case. This line of argument is quite similar to Hume's argument that future will resemble the past. The character of induction here is not logical and it cannot be justified rationally or logically. Following Hume, we may say that to work in such a way is the very meaning of our human nature. Induction is an original-natural tendency. Since the science of physics itself presupposes such an extension of the past to the future, Kant is not quite right in quoting this science in support of his thesis.

If, on the other hand, we are ready to accept our hypothesis aiming at a constructive and cooperative solution of the problem lying between Kant's criticism and Hume's naturalism, we must not then hesitate to conclude that the so-called logical and transcendental certainty and necessity which Kant speaks of are either fully formal or more or less natural in the Humean sense of the term. If we maintain the first alternative, then the entire subject-matter of the critical philosophy would belong to the field of Hume's relations of ideas. But this is what Kant's critical philosophy wants to avoid. And Kant's "Critique of Judgment" is the very bridge between his two other "Critiques".

Compared to and contrasted with Kant's criticism, Hume's naturalism lacks the conceptual clarity possessed by Kant's critical philosophy. This results in the more powerful conceptual frame-work which Kant's critical philosophy has at its disposal. The terminological strategy which is displayed by Kantian criticism is not to be found in Humean naturalism. As examples we can cite Kant's very neatly worked out theory of imagination. The way Kant solves the problem of unity is also better than the manner in which Hume does the same. Hume himself is very conscious of this imperfection in his presentation and he tells us this over and over again when he develops his theory of belief, an act which so pervasive in its effects that hardly any philosopher thought it worth the trouble to discuss. "This operation of the mind, which forms the belief of any matter of fact, seems hitherto to have been one of the greatest mysteries of philosophy: tho' no one has so much as suspected, that there was any difficulty in explaining it. For my part I must own, that I find a considerable difficulty in the case; and that even when I think I understand the subject perfectly, I am at a loss for terms to express my meaning . . ."[28]

Although Kant's criticism claims to be completely free from psycho-

[28] D. Hume: *Treatise*, p. 628.

logical elements, our comparative critical discussion has tried to show that this is not always the case. The so-called transcendental necessity and universality are, in the last run, based on our biological and psychological constitution. And Kant is right to assert that any mind similar to our own must know and act as we do.

Kant's critical philosophy tries to solve problems which belong to the field of matters of fact where truths are not formalized results. Kant's philosophy is unthinkable without guaranteeing the existence of synthetic judgments a priori. Our interpretation of Kant's critical philosophy has tried to show that we may accept the claims of Kant without necessarily accepting his method of justifying and explaining these claims. And this means that we may show that there are synthetic a priori judgments but that their a priori character is based on human constitution. Thus the Kantian a priori, according to our interpretation is a "constitutional a priori". Philosophers like B. Russell go still further and maintain that Kant's philosophy represents some version of pre-Humean rationalism and can be refuted by Hume. We have tried to show here that Kant's philosophy may be brought nearer to that of Hume, if we are ready to accept that there is a very fundamental relativity of all we think and do to the special human constitution.

Although Hume's naturalism is not averse to all forms of apriorism, still Hume would not accept the transcendental a priori of Kant, for that would mean confounding the two fields of knowledge – the field of the relations of ideas and that of the matters of fact. In opposition to Kantian a priori which is too rigid, Hume's a priori is more flexible and can be termed imaginative or natural.[29]

The Humean principles of human nature are also not exactly the same as the Kantian categories of the understanding, although they have a very similar function to fulfil – the function of showing how we really come to have knowledge as well as experience. In opposition to Kant, who emphasizes the constitutive character of the categories, Hume lays more stress on the guiding nature of his principles. Hume's principles are less rigid and more open to correction and modification if the future course of human experience demands it. Kant, on the other hand, determines the nature of experience in such a way that he would deny any such future correction or modification of experience as such. Thus, much misunderstanding of Kant regarding his understanding of the philosophy of Hume centers round the concept of experience.

[29] Cf. R. A. Mall: *Humes Prinzipien- und Kants Kategoriensystem*, in Kant-Studien, Heft 3, 1971.

"Hume woke Kant", Passmore writes, "from his dogmatic slumber only sofar as to inspire him to construct the very kind of philosophical system to which Hume most objected."[30] Thus, there is no hard and fast rule to rigidly determine the course of human experience. Philosophers have been generally misled by a misplaced dichotomy between experience and reason.

Hume's naturalism seems to be more radical than Kant's criticism, for it does not take for granted the character of objectivity, necessity and universality as depicted in the natural and mathematical sciences. Kant, unlike Hume, has put to himself the task of giving a philosophical foundation and explanation of Newtonian physics and Euclidean geometry. Hume is more sensitive to the uniformity of nature which is the cornerstone of all sciences – moral as well as natural.

The main assertion of Kant regarding the central problem of causal principle is: "all that begins to exist or comes to be presupposes something whereupon it follows a rule." In order to substantiate this, Kant cites examples which tacitly presuppose the a priori character of the problem. Kant's example is: one can foretell that if somebody destroys the foundation of his house it would collapse. What appears to be a priori has already been "learned" somewhere and sometimes, except the tendency (the inductive tendency of human nature) of anticipation that it would also happen in the future. In some way or other, the known is the only mode to know the unknown. Thus, the central fact about the principle of causality is that it is the most original way in which our human nature works. The causal axiom is therefore not less but more than a hypothesis.

Both Hume and Kant are of the opinion that the principle of causality cannot be said to belong to the field of the relations of ideas. If we wish to avoid making causality a principle simply of axiomatic character, we must take the bull by the horns and ask the most radical question: What is the real nature of the "presumptive character" which accompanies all our talk of causality? What is the nature of that conviction that all that happens must have a cause? Is it not simply an "inductive presumption" motivated, nay reactivated, by the twin factors of constancy and coherence? And some type of constancy and coherence we always experience.

Both naturalism and criticism start from the conviction that no knowledge is possible unless we presuppose – at least in the manner of a working hypothesis – the uniformity of nature. Applied to the spe-

<hr>

30 Passmore: *Hume's Intentions*, p. 153.

cial problem of causality, it means that every experience has the tendency of anticipating its own future course. It is this original inductive anticipation which is both immanent and transcendent to our experience – immanent because it is induced by experience, transcendent because it is presupposed by experience. Strictly speaking, there is no rational or logical foundation of the uniformity of nature. In other words, it is senseless to ask why nature is uniform.

Kant's great fear seems to have been that if he accepts the Humean program regarding the problem of the categories, they would lose all necessity and universality. It is always putting the cart before the horse if one tries to prove the universal character of causality by arguing that otherwise the causal principle would lose all universality. But the fear of Kant is unfounded because Hume too pleads for the universal and necessary character of causality. He asks: "Why a cause is always necessary? He is not asking: Is a cause always necessary? He only tries to trace back this character of necessity to some original "impression" of reflection endowed with vivacity, immediacy and liveliness. It is this impression which he terms mental determination. And this mental determination is neither a fiction of our fancy nor a representation of an outer perception; it is rather the very active propensity of human nature. Thus, we see that Kant's fear of Hume's scepticism is in fact unfounded.[31]

The following points seem to follow from what has been said above:

1. If the transcendental method of Kant – the very core of his critical philosophy – remains true to its calling of a method and keeps itself away from any formalization or ontologization, then there seems to be two main possibilities open to it: either a) it can supply us only with hypotheses or b) it conceives the categories as principles which are logical systematization of the results of the sciences. Our interpretation favors b) and tries to show that the critical philosophy of Kant may be brought nearer to the naturalism of Hume. Inspite of this, Kant's criticism is far superior to Hume's naturalism, which lags far behind with regard to conceptual and systematic clarity.

2. Whether Kant's critical philosophy may be interpreted the way we have suggested in point 1 or not, it, at any rate, contains certain elements which must be understood as the results of our processes of generalization, abstraction, idealization from out of our psychological and biological course of experience. Hume on the

31 Cf. Paulsen: *Kant*, p. 206.

other hand only partially carries out his intentions that his principles are neither sensuous nor logical-rational but natural.

If Hume's inordinate tendency to sensualize all experience is made responsible for the falling short of his otherwise very valuable and original philosophical insights, then so with Kant who, due to his rationalistic heritage, possesses a strong weakness for intellectualizing all experience.

3. In opposition to Hume's naturalism, Kant's criticism is rather too uncritical towards the achievements of the sciences like physics and mathematics.

4. Our critical interpretations, comparisons and appreciations of naturalism and criticism have tried to work out the hypothesis that the character of necessity is in the last run some sort of "natural presumption" badly needed, whether we engage ourselves in natural or moral sciences.

5. Even Hume is ready to gladly accept that we need principles (categories) in order to spell out the sensuous manifold. He would only insist that the principles are neither really completely rational nor empirical but rather natural.

6. Point 4 brings out the programmatic features common to both naturalism and criticism. First, they represent a middle path between the two extremes of dogmatic rationalism and scepticism; and, second, they both give a non-sensuous and non-rational explanation and justification of the principles as well as categories.

7. Although Hume fell short of founding phenomenology in the sense of Husserl who credits him to be a precursor of this movement, still his system of the principles is more open to the future course of experience than is Kant's. This might be the reason for Hume's diffidence with regard to what he calls his "sceptical solutions".

8. From what has been said in point 7 it follows that Hume is less a precursor of Kant than of Husserl[32] and that the continental philosophors – especially in Germany – have, more often than not, read Hume through the eyes of Kant.

9. The most distinctive contribution of the new philosophy of criticism lies in the fact that Kant maintained there is a priori knowledge which is not purely analytic. Hume's naturalism was not very clear on this point and talked of a priori knowledge mainly in the field of the relations of ideas.

10. The strength and the weakness of Kant's philosophy lies in the

[32] Cf. R. A. Mall: *Experience and Reason*, Chapters 4, 6, 7 and 8.

rigorous character of his system.[33] Hume in his first "Enquiry," Section XII, Part III, asserts that there is no demonstration in the field of matters of fact. His fundamental proposition is that, "Whatever *is* may *not be.*" It is simply a descriptive knowledge that our nature, as much a fact of the existing world as anything, works like this. We cannot demonstrate that it will remain constant. The possibility that nature may change or modify its course never seems to have occurred to Kant. Of course, such a possibility, formally, is against the very spirit of Kant's conception of the a priori forms. Still he will have to suppose that the structure of mental constitution will not change. What is the real nature of this supposition regarding the unchangeability of nature?

[33] The well-known Kantian scholar Prof. Heimsoeth maintained a similar view in a private discussion with the author. The Kantian system is too neat to be always applicable.

CHAPTER V

HUME AND KANT ON THE PHILOSOPHY OF RELIGION

The phrase "philosophy of religion" has various denotations and connotations. It has been generally used as a philosophical defense of religious convictions – of natural as well as of revealed theology.

The term "philosophy of religion" is used here neither as a philosophical defense of natural or revealed theology nor as apologetics. It is just a philosophical thematizing of religion with the main aim of understanding the phenomenon "religion".

Hume and Kant both contribute to the proposition that moral worth does not depend on religion. This means, in other words, that naturalism as well as criticism represent the primacy of the practical over the theoretical.

We can talk of a "Copernican revolution" in ethics and religion not only in the philosophy of Kant, who first looked for a law which directly determined the will a priori and reversed the ordinary relation between the two disciplines of religion and morals, but also in the philosophy of Hume, who maintains "that when you pronounce any action or character to be vicious, you mean nothing but that, from the constitution of your nature, you have a feeling or sentiment of blame from the contemplation of it."[1] Thus, Hume is crusading against ordinary morality – the religious morality of the eighteenth century. He is in fact repudiating, very much in the spirit of Kant, the religious foundation of morality. Seen in this way, Hume too seems to support the autonomy of morality. But still Hume, unlike Kant, does not affirm that moral principles are self-explicable and purely independent of human nature. "All morality", Hume says, "depends upon our sentiments"[2].

Starting from his theory of knowledge and through to his philosophy of religion, Hume was always in search of patterns – patterns of human

[1] D. Hume: *Treatise*, p. 469.
[2] *Ibid.*, p. 517.

behavior. And his confidence in the consistency and uniformity of human nature backed him all the time. Human nature is, and remains for him, the last point of reference whether he engages his mind in the field of the theory of knowledge, or morals and religion. We have already seen Hume's naturalistic interpretation of human life developed at length in his "Treatise" and the two "Enquiries Concerning the Principles of Understanding and Concerning the Principles of Morals." His "Dialogues Concerning Natural Religion" also rests on a similar naturalistic interpretation of man. To be good does not *necessarily* mean to believe in God. This is one of the central insights of Hume which he shares with Hutcheson. This fundamental anthropocentricity governs Hume's religious philosophy. In his letter of 1740 to Hutcheson, Hume refers to this: "I wish from my heart I could avoid concluding that since morality, according to your opinion as well as mine, is determined merely by sentiment, it regards only human nature and human life."[3] The main point which Hume wants to make here is that: no moral judgments can be made entirely independent of human sentiments and desires, and they are not simply any sort of statement about some objective reality around us.

Hume is well aware of the complex activities lumped together under the capital of "religion" and "religious beliefs". He wanted to do justice – so far as it is possible – to all aspects of religion and that is why it is unjust to treat Hume simply as a village atheist. The eighteenth century was not, of course, very sincere in matters of religion and it has been said that its sins were vulgar and its virtues dull. And Hume was very well aware of these surface activities in religion.

Hume's critics are divided with respect to the question of his religious attitude. Some regard him as an out and out atheist; others have held that he did retain an intellectualized belief in God. In the opinion of the author, both these views seem to be wrong, for Hume is neither a metaphysical materialist nor one who rejects the problem of God outright. He tries to show that the debate between theism and atheism – if rightly considered – turns out to be a merely verbal one. We shall come to this point in the course of our discussion.

Hume like Kant is fully convinced that there is no rational demonstration of the existence of God. In his "Natural History of Religion" Hume sums up the matter: "We may conclude, that the Christian religion not only was at first attended with miracles, but even at this day cannot be believed by any reasonable person without one. Mere reason

---

[3] J. Y. T. Greig: (ed.) *The letters of David Hume*, Oxford, 1932, I, p. 40.

is insufficient to convince us of its veracity; And whoever is moved by faith to assent to it, is conscious of a continued miracle in his own person, which subverts all the principles of his understanding, and gives him a determination to believe what is most contrary to custom and experience.''[4] Hume's denial of miracles really means his denial of a religious basis of morality. And the problem of "God" must remain an enigma for the cognitive powers of human beings. But in his conception of the good life Hume remained a humanist and a utilitarian.

We know that Hume's interest in religion was life-long. In his famous essay "Of Miracles", Hume very much in the spirit of Kant criticizes bigotry and superstition. Hume attacks in his "The Natural History of Religion" two beliefs. One of these is the supposition that there is *one* God and this corresponds to universal instinct of human nature. Hume is more inclined to regard polytheism as more natural. The other object of Hume's attack is the conviction that the so-called "higher religions" have been socially beneficial. The worst effect of any organized religion is the subversion of sincerity.

But in the "Natural History", Hume is very careful to warn his readers that he is not attacking religion as such but only its vulgar forms. Hume is completely opposed, on moral grounds, to all varieties of traditional religion. And what remains for the human intellect to believe is some sort of innocuous and impotent "philosophical" theism.

The "Dialogues Concerning Natural Religion" are Hume's very important contribution to the subject of philosophical theology. The third part of Kant's "Critique of Pure Reason" together with Hume's "Dialogues" may be said to be the two very sustained analyses of the subject in the modern philosophy of religion. Hume was very reluctant to publish his "Dialogues".

Cleanthes and Philo agree that the sole basis of beliefs is experience and inferences based upon it. This also goes to explain the meaning of the phrase "natural religion". It is opposed to "revealed religion". Natural religion is used by eighteenth-century writers to refer to a set of beliefs regarding the Divine and His qualities. These writers claim that natural religion is not founded on faith or revelation, but on reason and experience. This is what Hume's "Dialogues" thematize. Pamphilus delimits the argument of the "Dialogues" in that he says the main question is not whether God exists, but rather his nature, attributes and powers. And once we can show that it is impossible to determine the

---

[4] D. Hume: *Dialogues Concerning Natural Religion*, ed. by H. D. Aiken, cf. Introduction of the editor.

nature and attributes of God, the question regarding his existence becomes more or less vacuous.

Although the different characters of Hume's "Dialogues" – Cleanthes, Philo and Demea – show clear-cut border lines, still it is difficult to judge Hume's own personal conviction on the most important question of religion. Demea is an exponent of an orthodox rationalism and apriorism in religion. Cleanthes advocates an enlightened form of philosophical theism. Philo seems to represent the careless sceptic who ultimately shows the vacuous nature of the religious hypothesis. Both Cleanthes and Philo are against the orthodox rationalism of Demea.

During a deathbed interview, Hume assured his biographer that "he had never entertained any belief in Religion since he began to read Locke and Clarke."[5] There is a lot of bewilderment regarding the judgments of others on Hume's sincerity on religious matters. Some say he was motivated by a lust of paradoxes (Beattie), others find that Hume was wanting in seriousness (J. S. Mill, Huxley). Many blame him for not taking care of the issue between theism and atheism. Reading his "Dialogues" very carefully, one is convinced that Hume in fact reached a point where the issue evaporated and became verbal and vacuous. Theism and atheism both vanish into naturalism.[6]

In his brief preface to his "Dialogues", Hume describes the three main characters as "the accurate philosophical turn of Cleanthes, the careless scepticism of Philo and the rigid inflexible orthodoxy of Demea."

Of all the arguments for the existence of God, it is the argument from design motivated as well as derived from the appearance of order in the empirical world which has always been the most popular theistic argument. And Cleanthes in fact starts his discussion with this very argument. A very early philosophical formulation of this argument can be traced back to Anaxagoras and Plato. But it is St. Thomas Aquinas who formulates the self-same argument in nearly five ways. In modern times, William Paley's analogy of the watch conveys the essence of this age-old argument. Hume's "Dialogues" criticizes this argument very thoroughly although Paley took no account of Hume's argument.

For Cleanthes, the world appears to be ordered in the manner of a great machine whose parts are so wonderfully contrived as to lead us

---

[5] James Boswell: "An Account of My Last Interview with David Hume, Esq.," in *Private Papers of James Boswell*, ed. by G. Scott and F. Pottle, Mount Vermon, 1931. Reprinted as Appendix A to the Introduction, N. K. Smith: (ed.) *Hume's Dialogues Concerning Natural Religion*.

[6] Cf. D. Hume: *Dialogues Concerning Natural Religion*, Part XII.

to the supposition of a great Artificer which is then the God of religion. But Hume in his classic critique of the design argument points out that not only our universe but any universe we may conceive of is bound to show the sign of design. Without a considerable degree of arrangements no adaptation is ever possible or conceivable.

Hume through the person of Philo shows the defective character of such an empirical analogy. The relation that holds between God as the Artificer and the world is presumably single, individual and without parallel. Consequently, we cannot speak of God as the cause of the universe in any intelligible sense. We might, Hume suggests, as well ascribe the origin of the universe not to a mind but to an act of generation. This defines Hume's naturalism, for he maintains that it is better to stop with nature as its own cause than to be driven to a regress of causes which leads us nowhere. Cleanthes could hardly give any reply to this except that he does not care to ask for the cause of this cause.

Hume's own suggestion lies in partly reviving the Epicurean hypothesis: the particles constituting the universe might come to develop a pattern if the time given for this development is unlimited. This is in fact Hume's naturalism or his naturalistic hypothesis. The Darwinian theory of natural selection is another very scientific formulation of the same argument. So Hume does not deny order but only the inference from it of an intelligence which goes by the name of God endowed with moral attributes.

Hume also criticizes the very weak analogies between the world and the human artifacts such as house or watch.[7] There is something of symbolism in these analogies, and symbols as we know are: "never true copies of anything outside. Provided we accept the argument as valid we hardly can derive the good powerful God of the Christian tradition."[8] This finite and imperfect world we live in hardly allows us to infer an infinite creator. The problems of evil and unhappiness are too tough to be reconciled with the perfection and good will of a designer.

The most relevant part of Hume's "Dialogues" is part X, for he presents here the Epicurean trilemma which endangers God as a moral agent. It is the very age-old problem of an impossible reconciliation between a good God and the presence of evil in the world. Hume asks: "Is God willing to prevent evil, but not able? Then is he impotent? Is he able, but not willing? Then is he malevolent? Is he both willing and able? Whence then is evil?"

The fatal attack of Hume's "Dialogues" is not so much against the

---

[7] *Ibid.*, Parts VI and VII.
[8] *Ibid.*, Part V.

existence of God but rather against the moral attributes he is supposed to possess. Thus, Hume is demolishing the very essence of natural religion which at his time meant a set of beliefs about God and his moral goodness derived from reason and experience. Demea and Cleanthes are advocates respectively of the arguments from an a priori reason and experience.

Philo's position against natural religion is his "moderate scepticism" and he is not a Pyrrhonist denying the very idea of evidence based sometimes on common sense. Philo is open to reason and experience if they can make their claims true to infer God's existence and his qualities.

There is a tension between the arguments from commonsense and from Pyrrhonism. And it is this suspense which, Philo maintains, cannot be resolved by any argument supported by the common sense. Philo triumphs here.

Demea says in Part II: "The question is not concerning the *being* but the *nature* of God." Philo fully agrees with this contention of Demea's. The question regarding the being of God is a question regarding the being of a principle as the original cause of the universe. Hume attaches less or no importance to the name we wish to give to this most original principle. This may be also the reason why Hume retained the term God in his discussion.

Although the problem of God as being the cause of the universe cannot be separated from his moral attributes, they must still be distinguished. The main dispute between theism and atheism is not whether God is the cause of the universe but whether God has some more attributes than the single attribute of being the cause of the universe. Philo, who in such a situation represents Hume, now goes on to show how we in fact ascribe to God certain other attributes which are highly esteemed by men as wisdom, goodness, perfection, design and so on. This is how we adore him and start accepting his wishes as commands for us. But this should not mislead us, Hume reminds his reader, to believe that those attributes which are infinitely superior to our own have any resemblance to the same qualities among men. What Philo in fact criticizes here is the anthropomorphic turn of human mind first to wish a perfection, associate certain qualities with it, personify it and then feel as if there were such a thing as "God". So long as humanity thinks anthropomorphically there is hardly any direct road to natural or revealed theology.

The second challenge of Philo refers to Cleanthes. "Our ideas reach no further than our experience. We have no experience of divine attributes and operations. I need not conclude my syllogism. You can draw inference yourself."[9] The strength of the above argument lies in its very simplicity of showing the bounds of human reason and experience. All that Philo wants Cleanthes to draw as an inference is that we cannot prove anything about God's nature. And what makes natural religion so reasonable are really the moral attributes we so "illogically" associate with him. It is here that Cleanthes answers Philo's challenge by invoking the famous argument from design. A further battle line between Philo and Cleanthes is drawn. Philo won't allow any anthropomorphism and Cleanthes cannot help using it. Demea as a dogmatist is unwittingly siding with Philo against Cleanthes. Hume shows a very fine dramatic balance which he successfully maintains throughout the "Dialogues".

The central point which Philo wants to impress on Cleanthes in Part X of the "Dialogues" is that he might realize how little is involved in the expression "God exists". Hume slowly but surely gives a particular turn to the whole argument of the "Dialogues" in order to convince his readers that the main issue between theism and atheism is merely a verbal one. "It seems evident", Hume writes in Part XII of his "Dialogues", "that the dispute between the sceptics and the dogmatists is entirely verbal, or, at least, concerns only the degrees of doubt and assurance which we ought to indulge with regard to all reasoning; and such disputes are commonly, at the bottom, verbal and admit not of any precise determination. No philosophical dogmatist denies that there are difficulties both with regard to the senses and to all science, and that these difficulties are, in a regular, logical method, absolutely insolvable. No sceptic denies that we lie under an absolute necessity, notwithstanding these difficulties, of thinking and believing, and reasoning, with regard to all kinds of subjects, and even of frequently assenting with confidence and security." After showing this structural similarity in the way a sceptic and a dogmatist argues, Hume passes the judgment that: "The only difference, then, between these sects, if they merit that name, is that the sceptic, from habit, caprice, or inclination, insists most on the difficulties, the dogmatist, for like reasons, on the necessity."

Those who criticize Hume for not having realized that God might have allowed for suffering, that is to say, for evil, for some other reason fail to realize the force of Humean argument with regard to his

<hr>

[9] D. Hume: *Dialogues*, pp. 142–43.

revival of Epicurean dilemma. Philo is very obstinate on the point of anthropomorphism and he asks: "In what respect, then, do his benevolence and mercy resemble the benevolence and mercy of men?"[10] If Cleanthes is not going to mix up human benevolence with that of God, Philo's argument carries much weight. Even if we accept, Philo argues further, a purpose and design in nature, it is well nigh impossible to see in what way it serves human beings and the animals.[11]

Cleanthes puts to Philo the most crucial question, a question which is very unsatisfactory even to a moderate sceptic like Philo. Philo is really not a disbeliever; he simply argues that there is hardly any direct and logically-experientially convincing way from human reason and experience to God and his moral attributes. "If you can prove ... mankind to be unhappy or corrupted, there is an end at once of all religion. For to what purpose establish the natural attributes of the Deity, while the moral are still doubtful and uncertain."[12] Before Philo answers Cleanthes, Hume very wittingly lets Demea jump into the argument. Demea interrupts and presents his theodocy. "The life (is) but a moment in comparison of eternity. The present evil phenomena, therefore, are rectified in other regions, and in some future period of existence. And the eyes of men, being then open to larger views of things, see the whole connection of general laws, and trace, with adoration, the benevolence and rectitude of the Deity ..."[13]

This framework of Demea's theodocy asks us to take an eternal and most comprehensive view of existence. On the one hand, it wants to persuade us that since we lack such a broader view of existence we are mistaken in thinking that we suffer. On the other hand, our view is so limited and narrow that we fail to realize that what we call suffering serves a greater good. In other words, his theodocy wants to show that either there is no evil or it is necessary.[14]

Hume's main argumentative strategy is to allow Cleanthes directly to criticize this position of Demea's. "The only method of supporting", Cleanthes summons Demea, "divine benevolence (and it is what I willingly embrace) is to deny absolutely the misery and wickedness of man."[15]

<hr>

10 *Ibid.*, Part X, p. 198.

11 Cf. *ibid.*

12 D. Hume: *Dialogues*, Part X. It is interesting to note that Cleanthes very much in the spirit of Kantian argument tries to show that moral duties must somehow be related to God. It goes of course to the credit of Kant to have interpreted our moral duties as God's commands.

13 D. Hume: *Dialogues*, Part X.

14 Berkeley generally thinks of evil as an illusion whereas Leibniz emphasizes its necessary character. Hume challenges both the positions.

15 D. Hume: *Dialogues*, Part X.

Hume has nicely preplanned these two characters – Demea and Cleanthes. They generally criticize each other's position. And Philo is there to profit from it. Philo turns the very argument which Cleanthes uses against Demea against the general position of Cleanthes. "Admitting your position", Philo comments, "which yet is extremely doubtful, you must at the same time allow that, if pain be less frequent than pleasure, it is infinitely more violent and durable ... But not to insist upon these topics, I must use the freedom to admonish you that you have put the controversy upon a most dangerous issue, and are unawares *introducing a total scepticism into the most essential articles of natural and revealed theology.* What! no method of fixing a just foundation for religion unless we allow the happiness of human life, and maintain a continued existence even in this world, with all our present pains, infirmities, vexations, and follies, to be eligible and desirable! But this is contrary to everyone's feeling and experience; it is contrary to an authority so established as nothing can subvert ... by your resting the whole system of religion on a point which, from its very nature, must for ever be uncertain, you tacitly confess that that system is equally uncertain." Philo still goes further and pushes Cleanthes into a tight corner. "But allowing you what never will be believed ... Why is there any misery at all in the world? Not by chance, surely. From some cause then. Is it from the intention of the Deity? But he is perfectly benevolent. Is it contrary to his intention? But he is almighty. Nothing can shake the solidity of this reasoning, so short, so clear, so decisive, except we assert that these subjects exceed all human capacity."[16] This in short, is the position of Philo. Religion is a topic to which our common measures of truth and falsehood do not apply. Philo charges Cleanthes to have willingly rejected this contention which he asserts to have maintained from the very beginning.

Thus, Philo's position is as follows: (i) we cannot know anything about the attributes of God (about his nature); (ii) it must forever remain an anthropomorphic move if we ascribe only good qualities – natural as well as moral – to God; and (iii) the main issue between theism and atheism can be solved verbally rather than from arguments whether our point of departure be human experience or reason.

Thus, what Hume says regarding the possibility as well as impossibility of a natural religion amounts virtually to a denial of religion. He keeps using both the terms "God" and "religion" in his philosophy. His naturalism shows the limitations of human powers and faculties.

[16] *Ibid.*

But his naturalism itself cannot be understood as a proxy to religion. The use to which the terms "God" and "religion" are subjected is contrary to any in which they are generally used. "He (Hume) has himself no belief in miracles nor consequently in a special revelation; he has no belief in an after-life or in any type of specifically religious duties; he has no belief in a divine being to whom moral attributes can be ascribed and none therefore in 'God' as religiously understood."[17]

Hume is very particular to inform his readers that he is not against "true religion" which he allows because it has no such pernicious consequences as insincerety. But then the problem is that "we must treat of religion as it has commonly been found in the world, nor have I anything to do with that speculative tenet of theism which, as it is a species of philosophy, must partake of the beneficial influence of that principle ..."[18]

Hume is therefore a votary of philosophical religion, but his philosophical theism is, for all practical purposes, against the introduction of a transcendent God to whom moral attributes are ascribed. Whether Hume would accept the introduction of an "immanent God" is a matter of further interpretation.

If Hume's "Dialogues" has any winner at all it can be only Philo for it is he who argues till the last that either the moral attributes of God are at stake or the system of natural as well as revealed theology is uncertain.

There is a very characteristic passage in the "Dialogues" which shows that both Demea and Cleanthes at last come to realize that throughout Philo has been clever enough to have witnessed a fight between them feeling all the time that there is hardly anything to fight about. There are four hypotheses which can be framed with regard to the first cause: it is endowed with perfect goodness; it has perfect malice; it has both goodness and malice; and it has neither goodness nor malice. The fourth, Hume concludes, seems to be the one which is by far the most probable. Demea is suddenly alarmed when he hears Philo betraying the holy cause. "Hold! hold! cried Demea: Whither does your imagination hurry you? I joined in alliance with you in order to prove the incomprehensible nature of the Divine Being, and refute the principles

---

[17] N. K. Smith: *Hume's Dialogues*, Introduction, pp. 19–20. This clearly brings forth the deep-rooted temperamental, intellectual and philosophical differences between Hume and Kant – Kant, contrary to Hume, is convinced of having saved the moral attributes of God. Hume would see some type of underhanded dealings in Kantian argument, from the autonomy of morals to the practical necessity of religion.

[18] D. Hume: *Dialogues*, Part XII.

of Cleanthes, who would measure everything by human rule and standard. But now I find you running into all the topics of the greatest liberties and infidels ..." Cleanthes, who seems to have seen through Philo's game, comes to Demea's help. "And are you so late in perceiving it? replied Cleanthes. Believe me, Demea, your friend Philo, from the beginning, has been amusing himself at both our expense ..."[19]

To Hume and Kant goes the credit for having shown once and for all the very tenuous character of all our intellectual and rational bases of our belief in a transcendent God endowed with moral qualities. In spite of this very important programmatic and strategic similarity which is mainly negative in character, Kant's philosophy of religion within the limits of reason alone, unlike that of Hume, took on a completely different turn. God is introduced by Kant as a practical moral postulate so that the dictates of the moral law along with the possibility of their fulfilment may be guaranteed. The God of Kant takes over the role of a guarantor and the proper office of religion is to regulate the heart of men, humanize them and motivate them to be morally good. The religious critics of Kant fear that if the sole job of religion is to enforce the motives of morality it is well in danger of being overlooked and dethroned.

Two stages may be distinguished in the development of Kant's philosophy of religion: before the "Opus Postumum" and since and after the "Opus Postumum". The first stage of development is characterized by the most fundamental concept of the "highest good". This is the rational ideal of the complete and perfect human life. This concept has two ingredients: virtue and happiness. The former stands for our moral worth to be attained through obedience to the unconditional moral law; the latter represents the condition of a rational being in the world such that in the existence of such a being everything goes according to the will. Virtue is of course more important than happiness. Although virtue is the supreme good, it cannot be said to be the complete and the perfect good. And Kant maintains that the conception of the highest good requires both virtue and happiness.

The crucial problem for Kant is to show how this combination of virtue and happiness can be attained. We can be virtuous just by following the moral law and this means that virtue is an act of the will. But happiness depends also on the order of nature. And we know that the causality of nature is of a different order. "Hence there is not the slightest ground in the moral law for a necessary connection between

<hr>

19 *Ibid.*, Part XI.

the morality and proportionate happiness of a being which belongs to the world as one of its parts and thus dependent on it."[20] This leads Kant to postulate the existence of a cause itself different from nature, but a cause which brings about the combination of virtue and happiness. This cause is God.[21]

For Kant, then, it is a *moral necessity* to postulate the existence of God. This postulate represents a subjective rather than an objective necessity. And Kant feels that this moral necessity is enough to prove the existence of God. Kant affirms that this moral proof for the existence of God is superior to any other proof we can think of. If God's existence could be proved theoretically we must adjust our morals in accordance with theology. And such a position would imply a reversal of Kant's whole moral philosophy.

In his first "Critique" Kant hardly talks of the nature of God and of the future state of man, for he is mainly interested in showing the limit of human knowledge. Regarding the future state of man, Kant writes in his "Religion Within the Limits of Reason Alone": "We know nothing of the future, and we ought not to seek to know more than what is rationally bound up with the incentives of morality and their end."[22] But in his lectures on the philosophy of religion, Kant maintains that man should not expect a radical change in the next life. "Rather, experience of his state on earth and the ordering of nature in general gives him clear proofs that his moral deterioration ... as well as his moral improvement ... will *continue endlessly, i.e. eternally*" (italics mine).[23]

Unlike Hume, Kant ascribes to God moral attributes which are necessary for his role of guarantor of the highest good. "This Being must be omniscient, in order to be able to know my conduct even to the most intimate parts of my intention in all possible cases and in the entire future. In order to allot fitting consequences to it, He must be omnipotent, and similarly omnipresent, eternal etc. Thus the moral law, by the concept of the highest good as the object of a pure practical

[20] "Critique of Judgment," Schriften V, p. 124, Beck, trans. p. 228.

[21] It is interesting to contrast Kant's notion of causality with that of the Buddhist philosophy or with that of the "Rta" tradition in Indian thought. Unlike Kant the latter imagine an impersonal law which combines lawful character with just distribution. This means that one can accept Kant's frame of arguments without necessarily accepting his introduction of an intelligence called God.

[22] Greene and Hudson (trans.), p. 149n.

[23] K. H. L. Pölitz: (ed.) *Vorlesungen über philosophische Religionslehre*, Leibzig, Carl Friedrich Frans, 1917, p. 150, Quoted also by F. P. Van De Pitte: *Kant As Philosophical Anthropologist*, pp. 85–86. Kant here comes very near to the Hindu conception of an endless character of human life and of the world.

reason, defines the concept of the First Being as that of a Supreme Being."[24] Kant emphasizes over and over again that one could reach such a conception of the Supreme Being not through theoretical but only through practical, moral application of our faculties. God is the only being that is fully blessed. Kant strictly chooses only moral properties in God while discussing the relation of man to God. God "... is the only holy, blessed, and the only wise being, because these concepts of themselves imply unlimitedness. By the arrangement of these He is thus the holy lawgiver (the creator), the beneficent ruler (and sustainer), and the just judge."[25]

This trio of attributes is what makes God an object of religion. He is adored because of these qualities. Inspite of these seemingly very religious turns of Kant's mind, he always reminds us that our duty is not to please God but to obey the moral law which makes us virtuous. And provided we are virtuous in this God will reward us with happiness. Kant is thus vacillating in his resolution to purify the conception of God of all anthropomorphism and to represent him in a more human fashion in order to make him more forceful in our moral life. Human motivation seems thus to take an overhand on his strict moral teaching. He asks in his "Philosophy of Religion": "Why should I make myself worthy of happiness by means of moral conduct if there exists no being who can secure me this happiness?"[26] If our need to be satisfied cannot be fulfilled, how can morality command us. Kant has been variously accused of hedonism, utilitarianism and of having instrumentalized virtue. Although such a conclusion is not completely baseless it is not well founded. That it is not well founded can be seen by taking into consideration Kant's very radical and strict interpretation of the relation of man to the moral law in the "Opus Postumum".

Adickes' elaborate and careful study of the manuscripts composing[27] what is now known to be the "Opus Postumum" has done a great deal of service to the students of Kant in clarifying matters of great importance. To these matters of great importance also belongs Kant's philosophy of religion. The different sections of the "Opus Postumum" must have been begun not later than 1797. Kant seems to have departed from his former positions so far that authors like Vaihinger hold that Kant did accept the fictional character of all noumenal things including Divine Existence.[28]

[24] *Critique of Practical Reason*, Schriften V, p. 124, Beck, trans. p. 242.
[25] *Ibid.*, p. 131n.
[26] K. H. L. Pölitz: (ed.) *Vorlesungen über die philosophische Religionslehre*, p. 129
[27] Cf. Erich Adickes. *Kants Opus Postumum, dargestellt und beurteilt*, Berlin, 1920.
[28] See Appendix C, N. K. Smith: *Commentary*, 2nd. ed., 1923.

Kant seems to have gone to the opposite extreme in his closing years for he finds his former practical (ethical moral) proof for the existence of God unsatisfactory. And he insists that a more rigorous and consistent proof in accordance with the moral law must be forwarded for the existence of God.

If we accept that one of Kant's final positions, as revealed in his "Opus Postumum", is that our self can know things, i.e. function as a knower, only if it be a creator, then we must also accept the "as if" character of all the religious categories. But this does not mean any breach between Kant's first "Critique" and his "Opus Postumum". There is of course a continuity in his philosophical thought, for he remained true to his belief in the existence of things in themselves. It is only that in "Opus Postumum" the problematic character of the things in themselves comes more to the forefront than in any other works of Kant.

The passages which deal with the idea of God in "Opus Postumum" date from the years 1800–1803. Kant has the same attitude towards the idea of God as towards the concept of things in themselves. He is fully convinced that God exists: he is also convinced that nothing can be said about God. Kant's proof for the existence of God as found in the forward of his "Critique of Practical Reason" refers to the "Summum bonum", the highest good whose guarantor God is. This proof is no longer tenable for Kant in his "Opus Postumum". In order to eliminate from his ethical system all elements of hedonism and utilitarianism, Kant subjected his former theory to a more rigorous scrutiny. This means that man must act solely out of regard for the categorial imperative which is the only command which man has to follow and must follow. Kant has nowhere mentioned this radical change of mind, but the way he treats problems such as God and his relation to the moral imperative betrays that he is substituting the former proof for the existence of God with a proof of a more strictly moral character. N. K. Smith gives a threefold tentative formulation of this new proof and we may summarize it here.

1. Kant maintains that the religious interpretation of all duties as commands of God is not a supplementary, later interpretation, but is, for every moral being, immediately and necessarily given together with the apprehension of the duties. This means that the categorial imperative leads directly to God. "In the morally practical Reason lies the categorical imperative, to regard all human duties as divine commands. The realism of the Idea of God can be proved only through the duty-

imperative. Beings must be thought which, although they exist only in the thoughts of the philosopher, yet in these have morally practical reality . . .[29] A being which is capable of holding sway over all rational beings in accordance with laws of duty (categorical imperative), and is justified in doing so, is God. But the existence of such a being can be *postulated* only in a practical reference, namely (in view of) the necessity of so acting as if in the knowledge of all my duties as divine commands (*tanquam non ceu*) I stood under this awful but also at the same time salutary guidance and surety. Accordingly the *existence* of such a being is not postulated in this formula; such postulating would be self-contradictory.''[30]

There is a certainty of practical belief which Kant always insists upon. But the character of this belief is far from being clear.

2. Kant makes no reference to the existence of God but only to the idea of God. He nevertheless affirms that duties are to be apprehended as divine commands. "The categorical imperative of the command of duty is grounded in the Idea of an *imperantis*, who is all-powerful and holds universal sway (formal). This is the idea of God. What constrains us to the Idea of God? No empirical concept; no metaphysics. What presents this *a priori* concept is Transcendental Philosophy, the concept of duty. The imperative of duty proves to men their freedom, and at the same time conducts them to the idea of God.''[31]

3. Kant suggests in another passage of his "Opus Postumum" that God Himself, and not merely the Idea of God as a trans-subjective Being, is immanent in the human spirit. "God is not a being outside me, but merely a thought in me. God is the morally practical self-legislative Reason. Therefore only a God in me, about me, and over me. The proposition: There is a God says nothing more than: There is in the human morally self-determining Reason a highest principle which determines itself, and finds itself compelled unremittingly to act in accordance with such a principle. God can be sought only in us. There is a God, namely, in the Idea of the morally practical Reason which (determines) itself to a continuous oversight as well as guidance of the actions according to *one* principle, like to a Zoroaster.''[32]

---

[29] Such contentions of Kant are cited by Vaihinger in support of his "as if" interpretation of Kant's philosophy (Vaihinger: *Philosophie des Als Ob*). Interpreting Kant, we may assert that there is a very pregnant sense in saying that irrespective of what is the case with regard to the existence of God we always believe in the "*Idea* of God."

[30] See Appendix C, N. K. Smith: *Commentary*, p. 639.

[31] *Ibid.*, p. 639.

[32] *Ibid.*, pp. 639–40.

It is clear that Kant's views have undergone considerable change since the writing of the "Critique of Practical Reason". Not only the concept of the "summum bonum", the highest good, cannot afford surety, but even the mention of happiness would vitiate the purity of the moral law. Kant's interpreters, like Rosenkranz, go so far as to maintain that Kant identified religion with morality and "fell into the one-sidedness of absorbing religion in morality."[33] Kant in the views of these authors has deprived man of God in the traditional sense. And this interpretation gets some weight if one emphasizes only the immanent character of God, namely, God in me and not outside me. But a careful reading of Kant's "Opus Postumum" would convince us that this view is erroneous. Kant actually seems to reduce religion to a subcategory of morality because God is ultimately the very inner instance called moral self-determination. But such a reading of Kant must remain tentative for Kant himself emphasizes that morality leads to religion and this means that he is neither in favor of identifying religion with nor making it a subcategory of morality.

Kant leaves himself open to interpretations which are contrary. And the tension remains between the following two opposite readings of Kant's religious philosophy: (i) God as one who makes the coincidence of virtue with happiness possible and (ii) God as the very voice of the categorical imperative. The latter possibility is one which is of course hinted to by Kant but unfortunately is not fully worked out by him.

Kant's interest in religion seems to be life-long but religion is never allowed to assume an independent importance from morality. Although theologicians, like Karl Barth,[34] take Kant to task for having intended merely an anthropology in the name of a theory of salvation, still Kant seems to be sure that nothing glorifies God more than that which is most respected in the world, namely, the Divine Commands.

Although Kant never mentions the name of Hume in his "Religion Within the Limits of Reason Alone", he seems to have been acquainted with Hume's "Dialogues". Kant, very much in the spirit of Hume, denies the possibility of a rational theology and he must have read Hume's "Dialogues", for in 1780 the manuscript of Hamman's trans-

---

[33] K. Rosenkranz and F. W. Schubert: (ed.) *Immanuel Kants Sämtliche Werke*, 12 vols., Leipzig, 1838–42, XII, p. 202. Quoted in F. P. van De Pitte: *Kant As Philosophical Anthropologist*, p. 88.

[34] Karl Barth comments on Kant's doctrine of salvation and says that it "is intended to be anthropology and nothing but anthropology, even if it does have as its background a metaphysics with an ethical foundation" (*Protestant Thought from Rousseau to Ritschl*, trans. B. Cozens, New York, 1959, p. 187).

lation of Hume's "Dialogues" brought them to Kant's notice. It is quite strange that Kant consciously overlooks Hume's achievements in the philosophy of religion. Here too, the reason behind his not referring to Hume seems that Kant had already set up his edifice of philosophy and refused to be thoroughly disturbed by Hume.[35] It is Hume's anthropology[36] which hinders Kant from absorbing Hume completely. And we know today that Kant conceived his philosophical anthropology very early in his philosophical career and it is not out of place to remark that even his critical philosophy was influenced by and made to correspond to this anthropology.

The "Critique of Pure Reason" teaches us that the idea of God has no theoretical objectivity; it is not knowledge. So far, Kant goes with Hume. But Kant wants to make room for faith. And by calling the idea of God a postulate of practical reason he relates the whole problem of God with the moral law. The relation between morality and religion is reversed in that the morality becomes the basis of religion.

Kant's theology is completely ethical; it is an "ethico-theology". We have already seen that his ethical argument for the existence of God starts from the moral autonomy of man. The highest good is what complete morality implies, and complete morality consists in obeying the moral law. God, as we have shown, has to be postulated – at least this is what Kant's philosophy or religion demands before the "Opus Postumum" – as the guarantor for the coincidence of our moral worth with its most natural result, namely, happiness. Unlike Kant, Hume bases his ethics on humanitarian consideration of values.

Kant's philosophy of religion is contained mainly in his three works: "Critique of Pure Reason", "Critique of Practical Reason "and "Religion Within the Limits of Reason Alone". The last verdict of the first "Critique" is that there is no rational theology. But it does not mean the vacuousness and absurdity of religious conceptions like God, soul etc. They may not be knowable but they are still thinkable.

The "Critique of Practical Reason" tries to give some content to the ideas of reason. It tries to link the highest good with the moral law. This in its turn defines what we may term Kant's "rational faith" and belongs to the domain of the philosophy of religion.

The very first sentence of "Religion Within the Limits of Reason

---

[35] "The temporal priority," Van De Pitte says, "of the anthropology lectures (in relation to the Critical Philosophy) leads one to suspect that there may be causal priority as well ..." (*Kant As Philosophical Anthropologist*, p. 5).

[36] Cf. R. A. Mall: *Hume's Concept of Man – An Essay in Philosophical Anthropology*, pp. 130 ff., 156 ff.

Alone" provides us with the central theme of the whole book. Kant maintains – and he seems to anticipate his doctrine in the "Opus Postumum" – that morality is neither in need of a being above man to tell him what is his moral duty nor of another motive apart from that which is necessarily there in the principle of the categorical imperative. This means that morality does not need religion for its own sake; the need of religion is there because morality implies it.

Kant cannot base morality on the command of God for that would make his ethics heterogenous. And Kant is an uncompromising critic of all such ethical systems. Religion is, according to Kant, our knowledge of all our duties as Divine Commands. Morality unavoidably leads to religion. This is a proposition which Kant always believes in. In order to show the passage from the moral law to religion Kant concentrates on the "demand-character" of our moral law, for otherwise there is no fulfilment of the highest good. This is also the passage from his answer to his second question "What ought I to do?" formulated in his lectures on logic to answer his third question "What may I hope?" God thus becomes the fulfilment of a demand we necessarily feel within ourselves.

Happiness and moral excellence are not the same thing. This means that we cannot infer their correlation from the very concepts. Still their correlation is, Kant maintains, an a priori fact (morally). The character of necessity demanding the realization of the highest good is practical. The three postulates – immortality, freedom and God – define and determine Kant's theory of the postulates.

We have already seen that God is a moral legislator outside man. Between the two facets of the postulate of God within and outside man there seems to be a logical gap which is obstinate enough not to be bridged even by ethical arrangements. And Kant seems to opine that an act of faith is required to close this gap. Overemphasis on this act of faith has led many Kant interpreters to the view that Kant is underrating the all–importance of the moral law. But Kant is conscious of such a possible misunderstanding and he, therefore, asserts further that this act of faith is a moral necessity and the necessity to perform it arises within us as a rational demand of our practical reason. Thus Kant saves the autonomy of his moral law.

Kant is very particular in drawing a line of demarcation between creeds and religion. We can talk in plurals only with regard to creeds but not with regard to religion. Very much like Hume, Kant was also combating a certain kind of religion. Piety and bigotry are the two species of religious practices which in his lectures on Ethics Kant subjects to severe criticism. "Piety, which is practical, consists of obeying the divine laws for the reason that God wills it; bigotry is zeal in the worship of God which uses words and expressions of devotion and submission in order to win God's favor."[37] The only way to enjoy God's favor is by following the moral law, and when we obey the dictates of the moral law, God who acts in accordance with laws must favor us. Kant is fully against treating God as an earthly lord who must be pleased even if we have to flatter him.

But his criticisms of certain forms of worship do not imply his undermining the importance of the devotion of a truely religious man. "Devotion", Kant says, "is an indirect relation to the heart of God, which seeks to express itself in action to make the knowledge of God work effectively upon the will."[38] Thus, the purpose of devotion is to make us ready for action which is in accordance with the spirit of the moral law as well as God. Kant gives the example of a person interrupted in prayer by someone crying for need. To continue the prayer even after hearing someone crying for help is foolish, for the sole purpose of devotion lies in its being a means to some end. Devotion is not an end in itself.

Kant in opposition to Hume awards Christian religion a special place among religions. Hume was more doubtful about the special revelation the Christian religion is generally accepted to represent. Hume goes still further and points out with some sort of malicious pleasure that the tolerant pluralism of polytheism is in fact superior to the "implacable narrow spirit" of Judaism, "the bloody principles" of Mohammedanism and the "grotesque" intolerance of "modern" Christianity.

Both Kant and Hume deal with the proposition of how we can be good without necessarily believing in God? The apprehension of the moral law is independent of religion. And it seems that one can be moral without being religious. But one can be moral by being religious as well. A religious man will take the moral law as the command of God. And the fulfilment of this command would lead to the wished-for correlation between moral worth and happiness. But no one can be religious without being at the same time moral. This is the cornerstone of Kant's philosophy of religion and his whole life is a true application of this rule of conduct.

There is another way of showing how Kant is led to the postulate of God. God is the moral legislator endowed with all the moral properties,

<hr>

[37] See Van De Pitte: *Kant As Philosophical Anthropologist*, p. 90.
[38] *Ibid.*, p. 90.

e.g. all-knowing, all-powerful and benevolent. Kant was forced to distinguish between the apprehension of the moral law and its fulfilment. Since this fulfilment cannot be brought about by imperfect human beings there must be an instance that brings about this fulfilment.

The crux of the whole Kantian argument is this: He won't mind if we stop with the apprehension of the moral law and do our duty in accordance with the categorical imperative. But our stopping short of postulating God cannot explain the problem of the highest good. The still deeper rooted conviction of Kant is that if we obey the moral law we must be rewarded for that. Applying the "method of comparative difficulties" on what Kant says about the postulation of God, we may make the following remark: Provided we "postulate" God we can give a "more" satisfactory – if not the only satisfactory – explanation of the problem of the highest good and its realization by moral human beings. In case we do not "postulate" God it is more difficult – if not quite impossible – to give a satisfactory explanation of the same problem. In other words, if we are *only* moral and possess only virtue it is more difficult to explain and satisfy our moral demand for the coincidence of virtue with happiness. If we are both, moral and religious, we have less difficulty in satisfactorily explaining the same phenomenon. Consequently, morality necessarily leads to religion.

Irrespective of the truth and falsity of the Kantian postulate of God and irrespective of whether it can be interpreted in the sense of the fictional theory of Vaihinger[39] or not, this much seems to be certain: that had Kant put to himself the Humean dilemma with regard to the existence of God and the fact of evil in the world, he would have certainly undertaken a different standpoint in the domain of the philosophy of religion. Kant might rightly be suspected of being silent on the problem of evil, and Hume belongs to those philosophers of religion who demand from every philosophy of religion an answer to this problem.

[39] That the different ideas of reason lack any substantiality is Kant's own opinion. But it is also his firm conviction that we cannot do without them. Herein lies their theoretical unfoundedness and practical necessity. This leads to their synthetic a priori character in the field of our moral judgments. If we emphasize only the practical-pragmatic use of these ideas we may easily perceive Kant coming very near to James' philosophy of religion who too is convinced of the pragmatic value of religious concepts. Thus, Kantian God is not a substance but a value-concept. Vaihinger writes: "dass bei Kant noch eine radikalere Unterströmung vorhanden sei, durch welche die ontologische Substantialität jener Gegenstände in Frage gestellt wurde, wobei sich Kant mit aller Energie daran festhalte, daß der praktische Glaube an jene Gegenstände ein sittliches Gebot für den Menschen sei, daß er seine Handlungen in strenger Gewissenhaftigkeit so einzurichten habe, als ob jenen Gegenständen absolute Existenz vindiciert werden müsse ..." (H. Vaihinger: *Die Philosophie des Als Ob und das Kantische System gegenüber einem Erneuerer des Atheismusstreites*, Kant-Studien, vol. XXI, issue 1, 1917).

Another very important remark to be made with respect to Kant's philosophy of religion is that the moral law is a fact of human experience; it *is* there. This experience demands that virtue be rewarded with happiness. Kant seems thus to mix up the "demand-character" of our moral experience with the real possibility of its "fulfilment-character". Of course, it would mean a better moral construct if we postulate that there is or must be a God who serves the task of fulfilling this demand. Hume in a different context tries to show the impossibility of deducing the "ought" from the "is".[40] Kant's demand is practical, moral (subjective, formal) but the fulfilment must be conceived as material, real (factual, objective).

Suppose we maintain in the spirit of Buddhist theology that there is an impersonal law which is capable of bringing about the demanded coincidence of virtue with happiness, we would very well be in a position to grant all Kant's points without necessarily committing ourselves to his type of religious philosophy. The scope of this book hinders us in working out this hint of ours which could be of much use in the field of comparative religious philosophy.

Kant's "Weltanschauung" rests on the primacy of the practical over the theoretical. He, as an ethical voluntarist, seems to be led towards some type of dualism between duty and inclination. Since Kant is against all types of heteronomous ethics he introduces freedom which makes his ethics autonomous. But his postulation of God seems to involve another contradiction: Whereas in religion God is absolute, ultimate and autonomous, in Kant's ethics it is the moral law which deserves these predicates.

Kant's God is not something that *is* but something that *ought* to be, something that must be. And what ought to be as a demand of our moral sense must also, Kant affirms, exist. Kant substantiates his position further by arguing that in the absence of the postulate of God there would be no unity of purpose in nature and history. Thus, Kant's philosophy of religion is situated at the very cross section of moral law and teleology.

In his consideration of the maxims of moral actions Kant refers to teleological laws of nature. There is a systematic harmony of ends and Kant thinks that this can be explained and understood only when we regard maxims as teleological laws of nature. Hume too would not deny to accept such a purpose in nature but he would say that this is a hypothesis not fully supported by human reason and experience. Kant con-

[40] Cf. D. Hume: *Treatise*, pp. 469–70.

ceives of a complete conception of man which includes: (i) that man is a part of nature, (ii) that he is related to his fellowmen, (iii) that he is related to God and (iv) that he shares in a moral realm and transcends nature. Thus man is both a subjective and an objective phenomenon.

Kant's philosophy of religion seems to contain formal elements similar to his philosophy of morals. Moral goodness is as much a characteristic of the maxim entailed by the categorical imperative as the formal maxim of being worthy of God entailed by our accepting the moral duties as God's commands. What tempted Kant to postulate God is his conviction that such a postulate would easily explain the problem of our moral good which we can never conceive devoid of happiness. Kant failed to see that the wisdom he ascribes to God may just as well be ascribed to nature or to any impersonal law.

Our discussion has tried to show that, even if Kant's religious hypothesis is true, nothing of much consequence can be inferred from it. And this is exactly what Hume asserts in his "An Enquiry Concerning Human Understanding". Hume writes: "No new fact can ever be in-inferred from the religious hypothesis; no event foreseen or foretold; no reward or punishment expected or dreaded ..."[41] Hume personally is not against this or that religion. His difficulties are in regard to religion itself. He compares the drawback of religion, especially in its theistic forms, with that of the stoic ethics; both call upon man to live an artificial life.

In sum, both Hume and Kant deny the possibility of rational theology. Both further maintain that morality does not depend on religion. Thus, if by autonomy of morals we mean the denial of a religious morality we find Kant and Hume sailing in the same boat. But Hume unlike Kant bases morals on sentiments and sentiments alone and Kant unlike Hume on the categorical imperative.

Both Hume and Kant when they use the term "God" mean something quite different from what is ordinarily understood. Nevertheless, Hume makes explicit the quite negative character of his view regarding Divine Existence. Kant, on the other hand, ascribes to God moral properties which Hume would never dream of ascribing to Him.

Hume is convinced that religion when "true" and "genuine" has, at the most, the effect of rendering the mind immune to superstition and fanaticism. Kant expects much more from the acceptance of moral duties as Divine commands, for he thinks that would act as an incen-

---

[41] D. Hume: *Enquiries*, p. 146.

tive to us and give effect to the moral law. This is why Kant does not criticize all devoutness.

Like Hume, Kant too is an uncompromising critic of all creeds in the name of religion. No God and no religion can bestow upon us what we do not deserve. And the reason that we deserve something lies not in our flattery to God but solely in obeying the categorical imperative. Hume would like to know: If this is so, why postulate a God who in fact cannot do anything else than what he has to do as a result of our being virtuous which in turn results from our obeying the moral law. Unlike Hume, Kant seems to be fully convinced that moral excellence must lead to happiness. Kant feels that there is hardly any sense in possessing moral worth by means of moral conduct without at the same time having the guarantee that there exists a Being who can secure this happiness.[42]

Kant's God takes over the role of an executor, for he possesses only executive power. The legislative power seems to belong entirely to our moral autonomy. Kant's position is that moral goodness (virtue) necessarily entails reward (happiness). But the concept of reward cannot be analytically derived from our conception of moral goodness. Since we ourselves are not in a position to bring about this reward we must postulate God who performs this job. This is the answer by Kant to his third question, "What may I hope?" But this answer does not really solve the problem posed by Epicurean-Humean dilemma: How does it come that God, inspite of his omnipotence and benevolence, fails to bring about the necessary coincidence of virtue with happiness? In other words, how could we reconcile his existence with the presence of evil in the world.

We may fruitfully compare Kant's ethico-religious philosophy with that of Gita of the Indian philosophy. Both Kant and Gita preach the ideal of duty for duty's sake and represent anti-hedonism. But unlike Kant, Gita emphasizes the nature of our ethico-religious experience which goes to explain the non-formal and non-postulatory character of Gita's God. Kant of course would object and say that Gita gives up the autonomy of the moral law. But Kant's objection can be countered: For Gita, the so-called gulf between the religious and the moral experience does not exist at all, because Gita does not introduce God just to meet certain demands of our morality. God is just experienced (lived) as a totality wherein the imperative of duty for duty's sake retains its

---

[42] Kant did not realize that some type of philosophical theism in the sense of an enlightened humanism may as well explain our being virtuous without necessarily thinking of reward.

independence.[43] Thus, Gita's ethics offers us more than mere formal principles and Kant, when compared to Gita, seems to be half-hearted and stops short of founding the unity of the ethico-religious experience. The half-heartedness of Kant's philosophy of religion is of a twofold character. Kant is less bold than Hume in drawing the consequences which necessarily follow from his thesis of the moral autonomy, which reduces religion either to morality or makes it only a subcategory of it. Compared to Gita, Kant is not bold enough to revive the formal skeleton of his categorical imperative to life.

[43] Cf. S. Radhakrishnan: (ed., trans.) *The Bhagavadgita*, Chapter II, verse 47; Chapters XVIII, XVI, XII.

CHAPTER VI

TOWARDS A THEORY OF "ANTHROPOCENTRISM" WITH REGARD TO NATURALISM AND CRITICISM

From what has been said in the foregoing chapters, we may conclude that our interpretation aims at making Kant's criticism more "natural" and Hume's naturalism more "critical".

Not only the naturalism of Hume but also the criticism of Kant – if fully developed and understood – establish the thesis that Hume's and Kant's work can be understood as an anthropological system in the broad sense, i.e. a system with regard to the nature, place and destiny of man in the world.[1]

Unlike Kant, Hume does not use the term "philosophical anthropology". But the very introduction of his "Treatise" announces an all-comprehensive science of man and "'tis evident, that all the sciences have a relation, greater or less, to human nature ... Even *Mathematics, Natural Philosophy, and Natural Religion,* are in some measure dependent on the science of Man; since they lie under the cognizance of men, and are judged by their powers and faculties."[2]

Quite similar to Hume's view, Kant too formulates the four well-known questions of philosophy. "The field of philosophy, in this sense, may be reduced to:

1. What can I know?
2. What ought I to do?
3. What may I hope?
4. What is man?

The first question is answered by *Metaphysics*, the second by *Morals*, the third by *Religion*, and the fourth by *Anthropology*. In reality, how-

---

[1] For a detailed discussion of Hume's and Kant's anthropology see R. A. Mall: *Hume's Concept of Man – An Essay in philosophical Anthropology*; and Frederick P. Van De Pitte: *Kant As Philosophical Anthropologist.*

[2] D. Hume: *Treatise,* Introduction, p. XIX.

ever, all these might be reckoned under anthropology, since the first three questions refer to the last."[3]

This is a very clear and convincing formulation of the problem and importance of anthropology in a philosophic context. It also determines the relation of the four questions to one another and shows the all-importance of the fourth question which thematizes man as a whole.

Hume also speaks in the introduction to his "Treatise" of the four sciences dealing with logic, morals, criticism and politics. Compared to the sciences of mathematics, natural philosophy and natural religion these sciences have a closer connection to the fundamental science of human nature. Logic explains the principles and operations of the reasoning faculty and may be said roughly to correspond to Kant's first question. Morals and criticism, Hume says, regard our tastes and sentiments and may be said partly to correspond to Kant's second question. Politics considers men as members of society dependent on each other. This discipline may be said to correspond roughly to Kant's pragmatic anthropology. "In these four sciences", Hume writes, "of *Logic, Morals, Criticism, and Politics*, is comprehended almost everything, which it can any way import us to be acquainted with, or which can tend to the improvement or ornament of the human mind."[4] Very much in the spirit of Kant, Hume asserts that we can hardly hope to make progress in our different disciplines unless we are acquainted with this science of man. Very diffidently, Hume writes: "In pretending therefore to explain the principles of human nature, we in effect propose a compleat system of the sciences, built on a foundation almost entirely new, and the only one upon which they can stand with any security."[5]

In comparision to Kant's anthropology which is not only empirical and descriptive but also normative, i.e. essential and transcendental Hume's anthropology is mainly descriptive and natural.[6]

Hume's theory of man seems today to possess more "market-value" (Hendel) than many other theories about the nature of man and his destiny. Man is more natural and instinctive than rational. In opposition to Kant's view of man, Hume's concept of man is more naturalistic, and his guiding forces in human life are the forces of instincts, feeling, belief, imagination and sympathy. If Hume may be criticized

---

[3] T. K. Abbott: (trans.) *Kant's Introduction to Logic*, London, Longmans, Green, and Co., 1885, p. 15.

[4] D. Hume: *Treatise*, Introduction.

[5] *Ibid.*

[6] Cf. F. P. Van De Pitte: *Kant as Philosophical Anthropologist*, Introduction; R. A. Mall: *Hume's Concept of Man*, Introduction.

to have overrated the importance of factors like feeling and sentiment, Kant may be criticized to have underrated the importance of them. Both Kant and Hume accept and show in their philosophies the primacy of the practical over the theoretical. But their main difference lies in the manner they work out the implications of such a primacy. Hume establishes a naturalistic-descriptive anthropology; Kant establishes a descriptive-transcendental one.

From what has been said above, it should be clear that there is a general rule of the anthropocentrism at work in Hume's naturalism as well as in Kant's criticism.

The central thesis of our proposed anthropocentrism in naturalism as well as in criticism is the following: The fundamental principles of Kant's critical and Hume's natural philosophy – the categories and the principles – rest ultimately on a natural-factual foundation, to wit, the anthropocentric constitution of human mind. This means that both the systems are relative to the particular, i.e. peculiar, characteristic of the type of mind we human beings have. Thus the universality and necessity which are the distinguishing marks of the categories and the principles are relativized to the workings of the human nature. Thus the character of necessity and universality which these systems possess is, strictly speaking, a borrowed one; it is hypothetical (relative) and not absolute, for it can be traced back to the very natural and native ways our human nature works. Hume expresses it very clearly when he says that we follow our taste and inclinations not only in music and poetry but also in philosophy and that "nature has determined us to judge as well as to breathe and feel."[7] The way of her determination is labelled by Hume "absolute and uncontrollable". Thus the theory of anthropocentrism maintains that the most powerful determining factor in the natural philosophy of Hume and in the critical philosophy of Kant is the thorough subordination of their philosophical principles to the special constitution of human mind and nature.

Authors like N. K. Smith, C. W. Hendel, B. M. Laing, Metz and so on have convincingly shown that the naturalistic interpretation of the principles of human nature is the best possible way to understand and interpret Hume's philosophy. "My general conclusion will be", Smith writes, "that the establishment of a purely naturalistic conception of human nature by the thorough subordination of reason to feeling and instincts is the determining factor in Hume's philosophy."[8]

---

[7] D. Hume: *Treatise*, p. 183.
[8] "The Naturalism of Hume," in *Mind*, vol. XIV, 1905, p. 150.

Hume claims to have found in human nature, i.e. in its ways of working, the most ultimate point of all explanations and justifications. This project to work out a fundamental and foundational science equals any epoch-making revolutions in philosophy, and in this respect Hume may well be compared to Kant and Husserl.

To start with, the human nature Hume talks of is not biological nature – neither is it physical-physiological nature. The human nature he speaks of and whose principles he works out in his philosophy is the very center of all performances; it is, to use his own words "a foundation almost entirely new".

The human nature is given to us in and through the various principles of its own which represent the ways it works. The basis of human nature along with its original principles is the most secure foundation of all human inquiries. Hume, as an anatomist of human nature, conceives of a science which would mean a complete change in the systems of all other sciences. In the words of Price this may be termed the Scottish version in philosophy of the Copernican revolution.

All our investigations, Hume proclaims, must be carried out to lead us to the center of all the sciences, namely, to the human nature and its principles. Hume criticizes the old method of philosophical research as too speculative and "tedious". Hume proposes and follows the method of "experimental reasoning". Quite similar to the anonymous performances (anonyme Leistungen) of Husserl's transcendental subjectivity, Hume's nature guides us and helps us in our judgments in the different fields of our inquiries. "For me it seems evident", Hume writes in the introduction to his "Treatise", "that the essence of mind being equally unknown to us with that of external bodies, it must be equally impossible to form any notion of its powers and qualities otherwise than from careful and exact experiments, and the observation of those particular effects, which result from its different circumstances and situations. And tho' we must endeavour to render all our principles as universal as possible, by tracing up our experiments to the utmost, and explaining all effects from the simplest and fewest causes ..."

Hume is his own best critic and tries to meet a possible criticism which may be levied against him – that he accepts the impossibility of explaining ultimate principles. He says, if this be "esteemed a defect in the science of man, I will venture to affirm, that 'tis a defect common to it with all the sciences, and all the arts, in which we can employ ourselves, whether they be such as are cultivated in the schools of the philosophers, or practised in the shops of the meanest artizans."[9]

---

[9] D. Hume: *Treatise*, Introduction, p. xxii.

It is not the same thing to say (i) that there are ultimate principles which cannot be further explained and (ii) that these principles themselves are the ultimate principles of explanation. Hume characterizes human nature further by saying that it is the "original constitution" of human mind.

Besides the originality of human nature Hume also emphasizes its arbitrary character and thereby seems to mean that the ways of human nature "founding" all our inquiries cannot themselves be "founded". Hume refers here to the "primary constitution of human nature".

The nature Hume speaks of does not differ from man to man ; it is something which is common to all of us. The generality of anthropocentrism is established when Hume writes that "nature will always maintain her rights, and prevail in the end over any abstract reasoning whatsoever."[10] While explaining the original principle of habit, Hume clearly tells us that he only points out a principle of human nature "which is universally acknowledged, and which is well known by its effects."[11] The original propensity that lies at the back of such a principle of human nature cannot itself be ultimately explained.

Hume does not "hypostatize" the human nature as a Platonic entity. The functional-foundational sense of human nature makes it an "abbreviator" for the original ways our human nature works. Nature is not opposed to the principles guiding human life. The different principles of human nature characterizing Hume's naturalism represent "the accurate anatomy of human nature."[12]

Hume's theory of imagination and its "oblique" ways of working point out that the special constitution of our mind is the last basis of all the other fundamental principles. We have already seen that imagination is a permanent, irresistible and universal propensity in us and that Hume goes so far as to identify it with human nature as such.[13]

A careful reading of "Treatise", Book I, Part IV, Sections I and II – "Of scepticism with regard to reason" and "Of scepticism with regard to the senses", respectively – makes it sufficiently clear that the ultimate factual natural foundation of all our judgments and activities is the original constitution of human mind. Scepticism cannot be avoided if we make our point of departure in philosophy either the senses or reason and understanding. The only cure to all scepticism is the authority of human nature.

₁₀ D. Hume: *Enquiries*, p. 41.
₁₁ *Ibid.*, p. 43.
₁₂ D. Hume: *Treatise*, p. 263.
₁₃ *Ibid.*, pp. 225 ff.

In the field of morals we find Hume substantiating the same thesis of the universality of anthropocentrism. Moral judgments may be said to belong to the field of matter of fact but it is a matter of fact which is the object of feeling and sentiment and not of reason. Moral distinctions are not derived from reason.[14] The real seat of moral approbation and disapprobation lies in us and not in the object "so that when you pronounce any action or character to be vicious, you mean nothing, but that from the *constitution of your nature* you have a feeling or sentiment of blame from the contemplation of it (italics mine).[15] Morality is more properly felt than judged.

It was easier in the case of Hume to show and substantiate the thesis of anthropocentrism. We shall argue in the following lines that the universal and necessary character in Kant's Critical Philosophy can also be traced back to the specifically human context.

The forms of intuition in the Transcendental Aesthetic refer undoubtedly to *human* intuition. The way we human beings *intuit* is the only way we know of and this is the very anthropocentric character of our intuitional apparatus. Kant himself is very clear on this point: "But intuition takes place only in so far as the object is given to us. This again is possible, *for us men at any rate* (uns Menschen wenigsten) in so far as the mind is affected in a certain way. The capacity (receptivity) for receiving representations through the mode in which we are affected by objects, is called sensibility. Objects are given to *us* by means of sensibility, and it alone yields us intuitions" (A 19; B 33, italics mine). Kant says further that there is no other way in which objects can be given to us. And this means that the ultimate reference is to the very special constitution of the human sensibility which is anthropocentrically determined. In other words, there is a thorough relativization of the way objects are and can be given to us to the very original faculty of intuition. "Our nature is so constituted", Kant clearly tells us, "that our intuition can never be other than sensible ..." (A 51; B 75).

Kant of course denies whether creatures different from us (e.g. gods, angels) would intuit the way we do. But this is a point our thesis of anthropocentrism does not wish to thematize. The main point in favor of our thesis is that there is a subjective constitution of mind and the forms of intuition belong to it. This is why Kant calls space "the subjective condition of (our) sensibility, under which *alone* outer intuition

<hr>

[14] *Ibid.*, pp. 457 ff.
[15] *Ibid.*, p. 469.

is possible *for us*" (A 26, B 43, italics mine). Similarly time "is nothing but the subjective condition under which *alone* intuition can take place *in us*" (A 37; B 49, italics mine).

Quite similar to Hume Kant too starts from the fact that there is a common human nature. The only way of perceiving things we know of is our way of doing this – "a mode which is peculiar to us, and not necessarily shared in by every being, though, *certainly by every human being*" (A 42; B 59, italics mine). Kant of course speaks here of other beings and seems to entail that they might have other ways of intuition. But, strictly speaking, his very use of the concept of being betrays that either there is – at least partly – an anthropocentric extention of the concept of being to something – at least partly – similar to us or we have no way of obtaining information about this other "something". From what has been said above, it should be clear that the universality and necessity is relative to the special constitution of human sensibility.

The different categories of understanding bear a similar, specifically man-relative character. When Kant speaks of the understanding he always means our human understanding, and the forms as pure concepts of understanding are peculiar to it. Similar to the forms of sensibility representing the subjective conditions of our intuition the categories "represent *subjective conditions of (human) thought*" (A 89; B 122). The anthropocentric feature of the concepts of understanding can be established because Kant clearly maintains that the only way we can think objects is through the categories. Thus, their *a priori* character, on our interpretation, is ultimately their anthropocentric determination. That the forms of our sensibility as well as of our understanding are a priori, i.e. universal and necessary, means that they are relative to and grounded in the very special constitution of our mind.

Even the transcendental unity of apperception – the universality of the "I think" – resides in the specific constitution of the human mind. The faculty of the productive imagination works in an oblique manner and Kant, as we have already shown, repeatedly says that we cannot explain why it works in this way and not in any other way. He uses the term "inexplicable" (unerklärlich).

Quite similar to the human nature of Hume there is a corresponding manifestation of the constitutive features of the human mind in the philosophy of Kant. It must be accepted as an ultimate fact, incapable of further explanation, that our sensibility and understanding possess two forms and twelve categories respectively. Kant could hardly be more explicit on this point: "This peculiarity of our understanding, that it can produce *a priori* unity of apperception solely by means of the categories, and only by such and so many, is *as little capable of further explanation as why we have just these and no other functions* of judgment, or *why space and time are the only forms* of our possible intuition" (A 145; B 146, italics mine).

The Copernican Revolution – whether we speak of a Scottish version of it or the most explicit Kantian formulation – is, according to our anthropocentric thesis, the fact of an all-comprehensive relativization which is fundamental, foundational and ultimate in our search for explaining the ways of thinking, judging and doing things. Any philosophical system we can ever conceive of must accept this surd fact which may be termed the "anthropocentric a priori" and all other types of a priori are relative to it and derived from it.

The central teaching of Kant's "Critique of Judgment" is that we cannot help conceptualizing nature the way we do. And the way we conceptualize nature is to see purpose in her. Kant testifies to it when he speaks of a different kind of causality from that of the natural laws, namely that of purposes and final causes.[16] The human mind is so constituted that it cannot help seeing purpose in nature.

Since the category of purposiveness is something we bring to nature when we study her, the ultimate status of this category is regulative. We can, Kant maintains, conceive of other sorts of intelligences which do not conceptualize the nature the way we do, but "*for us men* there is only permissible the limited formula: We cannot otherwise think and make comprehensible the purposiveness which must lie at the bottom of our cognition of the internal possibility of many natural things than by representing it and the world in general as a product of an intelligent cause (a God) ..." After criticizing the theory that purpose, order and so on can be explained on the ground of mere mechanical principles of nature, Kant continues: "So much only is sure that if we are to judge according to what is permitted us to see by *our own proper nature* (the conditions and limitations of our reason), we can place at the basis of the possibility of these natural purposes nothing else than an intelligent Being. This alone is ... inseparably attached to the human race."[17]

It is very interesting to notice that both Hume and Kant accept the category of purpose and order in nature and relate this way of viewing the

<hr>

[16] I. Kant: *Kritik der Urteilskraft*, Section 77.
[17] *Ibid.*, Section 75 (quoted by N. Rescher: "Kant and the Special Constitution of Man's Mind," in: *Akten des 4. Internationalen Kant-Kongresses*, Part II, 1, p. 322–23).

world of nature to the very specific character of the human mind. At the same time it is no less interesting to see how they choose two quite different instances to which this order may be said to be due. In opposition to Kant, Hume maintains that we may stop with nature in our search for the most ultimate cause of order and organization. Both proceed in the anthropocentric manner but differ in their judgment regarding the problem of the final cause.

The way Kant introduces the postulate "God" in his philosophy of religion points out the necessary character (practical, moral) of this postulation. This means that it is a necessary regulative principle attached originally to our human nature, to our human point of view.[18]

The realization of happiness is specific to human life. Kant means to say that from the very nature of our constitution we cannot help asking "What may I hope?" after accomplishing the dictates of our moral law. That we ask like this must be accepted as a given ultimate in the ethico-theology of Kant and is incapable of further explanation. The following passage from Kant's "Critique of Judgment" specifies the anthropocentric bearing of what the categorical imperative amounts to and stands for: "It is clear, then, that it is owing to the subjective constitution of our practical faculty that the moral laws must be represented as commands and the actions conforming to them as duties, and that reason expresses this necessity, not by an "is" (happens), but by an "ought to be".[19]

It may be objected that our anthropocentric thesis misrepresents the transcendentalism of Kant's critical philosophy. How are we to know that the human mind has these and only these factual features? Don't we confound empirical method of inquiry with the transcendental method? Does not our factual inquiry depend on experience which vitiates the whole system of a priori truth?

In order to answer the above objections we must make it clear that the factual should not be confused with the empirical which it does not necessarily entail. If we base our factual understanding of our mind on experience (empirical) then of course we are guilty of confounding the factual with the empirical. But we maintain that the very possibility of understanding our experience of this or that thing rests on an ultimately peculiar characteristic of human mind.

In order to substantiate our thesis of anthropocentrism we take the help of a "naturalistic" method of working out the factual basis of our

[18] *Ibid.*, Sections 88 and 91.
[19] *Ibid.*, Section 76 (Rescher: p. 324).

fundamental principles. This natural method is non-empirical, non-transcendental and non-analytical. It is natural in the sense of being descriptively natural. It of course takes the help of observation and experiment but it does not construct. It is natural in the sense of being the most genuine and easy method of description with the end in view that we thereby arrive at the most original and factually foundational and fundamental principles of our inquiries in all the different fields. This is what we mean when we say that there is a "natural way" of bringing out the factual basis of the fundamental principles of Hume's naturalism and Kant's criticism. On our interpretation, the "transcendentality" of the so-called transcendental method would ultimately mean nothing but the very factuality of the surd fact of our human constitution and of the factual ways in which it works. The job of philosophy is to thematize this human nature and work out its principles which go to explain our thinking, feeling and doing the things we do.

A dogmatic Kantian would of course insist on a route to the discovery of the factual that is neither empirical nor analytical but a priori, which then in Kantian terminology would be the transcendental route. We feel that the problem of the route we take to discover the factual basis of our judgments in the different fields of our inquiries is not an integral part of the inventory of the critical philosophy.

The advantage of our suggested route to the factual basis of our judgments over the other routes mentioned here is essentially this: it does not dogmatically determine the whereabouts and the number of the principles, categories. It leaves the question open whether the categories are nativistic tendencies in us or have evolved themselves in the course of the development of the human mind.[20] This implies that the problem of a priori may as well be interpreted in a naturalistic-nativistic and evolutionary fashion. In opposition to the transcendental method which is averse to the "evolutionary epistemology" (Donald Campbell) the naturalistic method is not fixed and predetermined.

The crucial fact about all these methods is that they start from something which is given – in our context the a priori and its necessity and universality. We start from our a priori and try to find out the ultimate

[20] Konrad Lorenz writes: "Kant war offensichtlich der Überzeugung, daß eine naturwissenschaftliche Antwort auf diese Frage (die Frage nach dem a priori) prinzipiell unmöglich sei. In der Tatsache, daß die Anschauungsformen und Denkkategorien nicht ... durch individuelle Erfahrungen gebildet werden, mußte Kant den zwingenden Beweis dafür sehen, daß sie "denknotwendig" und damit überhaupt nicht im eigentlichen Sinne "entstanden," sondern eben a priori gegeben seien ..." (*Die Rückseite des Spiegels – Versuch einer Naturgeschichte menschlichen Erkennens*, p. 19).

basis it requires. In order to reach the factual foundation we first examine our experience and find that our experience is partly the result of the a priori factors. Consequently, it cannot be the ground of the a priori. Since Hume's understanding of the concept of a priori was too narrow, he denied a priori in the field of matters of fact. Kant, on the other hand, maintained the thesis that the a priori is a thought-necessity and can never be interpreted as something which has come to be what it is. We maintain that: (i) there is always an a priori and (ii) this is due to the fact of our possessing a human nature.

From what has been said above about the problem of the a priori (necessity), it follows that the necessity and universality – the all-encompassing anthropocentric character of necessity and universality – that we suggest and try to show as the ultimate factual basis of Hume's naturalism and Kant's criticism, is not logical, absolute necessity; neither is it a relative nor contingent necessity in the sense of conventionalism. It is not the necessity of the natural laws but, rather of the human nature in the sense of its contingency to the special constitution of the human mind. The following schematic representation of the different types of necessity makes our point still clearer:

NECESSITY

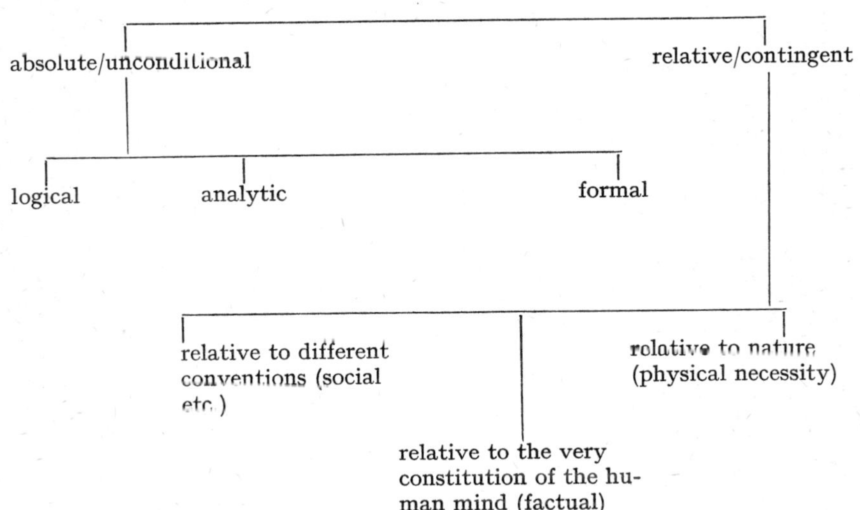

This tentative modal theory of necessity makes the complex structure of necessity clear and shows that there is some sort of isomorphism between the absolute and the relative types of necessity. Some sort of factuality is always at work – factuality in the sense of the ultimately factual basis of our judgements in the different fields of our human inquiries.

We have given a short and very imperfect sketch of our proposed theory of the universality of anthropocentrism and our intention has been to show the fundamental relevance of the general rule entailed by this anthropocentrism.

BIBLIOGRAPHICAL REFERENCES

List A contains only the primary sources – main works of David Hume and Immanuel Kant. List B includes only the names of such works as have been directly or indirectly alluded to in the course of the book.

LIST A

Hume, David: "An abstract of a Treatise of Human Nature," reprinted in *Hume – Theory of Knowledge*, ed. by D. C. Yalden-Thomson, Edinburgh, 1951.

—: *Dialogues Concerning Natural Religion*, ed. with an Introduction by H. D. Aiken, The Hafner Library Classics, number five, New York, 1966.

—: *Enquiries Concerning the Human Understanding and Concerning the Principles of Morals*, ed. by L. A. Selby-Bigge, London, 1966.

—: *Essays: Moral, Political and Literary*, Oxford University Press, 1963.

—: *The Natural History of Religion*, ed. by H. E. Root, London, 1956.

—: *The Philosophical Works of David Hume*, in four volumes, ed. by T. H. Green and T. H. Grose, London, 1875.

—: *A Treatise of Human Nature: Being an Attempt to introduce the Experimental Method of Reasoning into Moral Subjects*, ed. by L. A. Selby-Bigge, Oxford, 1960.

Kant, Immanuel: *Kants gesammelte Schriften*, ed. by Königlich preussische Akademie der Wissenschaften (23 vols.; I-VII, XIV-XVI Berlin: G. Reimer, 1905–1914; IX-XIII, XVII-XXIII Berlin: Walter de Gruyter & Co., 1922–1955).

—: *Kritik der praktischen Vernunft*, ed. by K. Vorländer, philo. Bibliothek, Bd. 38, Hamburg, 1959.

—: *Kritik der reinen Vernunft*, philo. Bibliothek, Bd. 37a, ed. by Dr. R. Schmidt, Hamburg, 1956.

—: *Kritik der Urteilskraft*, ed. by K. Vorländer, philo. Bibliothek, Bd. 39a, Hamburg 1959.

—: *Metaphysik der Sitten*, ed. by K. Vorländer, philo. Bibliothek Bd. 42, Hamburg, 1966.

—: *Prolegomena zu einer jeden künftigen Metaphysik, die als Wissenschaft wird auftreten können*, ed. by K. Vorländer, philo. Bibliothek, Bd. 40 Hamburg, 1957.

—: *Die Religion innerhalb der Grenzen der bloßen Vernunft*, ed. by K. Vorländer with an Introduction by H. Noack ("Die Religionsphilosophie im Gesamtwerk Kants"), philo. Bibliothek, Bd. 45, Hamburg, 1966.

—. *Vorkritische Schriften bis 1768*, Immanuel Kant, ed. by W. Weischedel, vol. 1, Darmstadt, 1960.

LIST B

Abbott, Thomas Kingsmill: (trans.) *Kant's Introduction to Logic*, London, Longmans, Green and Co., 1885.

Adamson, R.: "Hume" in *Encyclopaedia Britannica*, 9th ed., 1881.

Adickes, Erich: *Kants Opus Postumum, dargestellt und beurteilt*, Berlin, 1920.

Barth, Karl: *Protestant Thought from Rousseau to Ritschl*, trans. by B. Cozens, New York, Harper and Row, 1959.

Bauch, B.: *Parallelstellen bei Kant und Hume*, Kant-Studien, Bd. 19, 1914.

Beattie, J.: *Essay on Truth*, London, 1774.

Beck, Lewis. W.: *A Commentary on Kant's Critique of Practical Reason*, University of Chicago Press, 1960.

—: (trans.) *Critique of Practical Reason and Other Writings in Moral Philosophy*, University of Chicago Press, 1949.

—: *Studies in the Philosophy of Kant*, Indianapolis, Bobbs-Merrill Co. Inc., 1965.

Beck, L. W.: *Lambert und Hume in Kants Entwicklung von 1969–1772*, Kant-Studien, 1969.

Berger, G.: "Husserl et Hume," in *Rev. Int. de Philosophie*, I, 1939/40.

Berkeley, George: *Three Dialogues between Hylas and Philonous*, ed. by Colin M. Turbayne, The Library of Liberal Arts, 1957.

—: *A Treatise Concerning the Principles of Human Knowledge*, New York, 1957.

Bilharz, A.: *Descartes, Hume und Kant – Eine kritische Studie zur Geschichte der Philosophie*, Wiesbaden, 1910.

Boswell, J.: "An account of my last Interview with David Hume Esq.," in *Private Papers of James Boswell*, ed. by G. Scott and F. A. Pottle, vol. XII, Mount Vernon, 1931.

Brunius, Th.: *David Hume on Criticism*, Figura 2, Upsala, 1952.

Burton, J. H.: *Life and Correspondence of David Hume*, 2 vols., Edinburgh, 1846.

Cassirer, E.: *The Philosophy of the Enlightenment*, trans. by F. C. A. Koelln and J. P. Pettegrove, Boston, Beacon Press, 1955.

Cavendish, A. P.: *David Hume*, London, 1969.

Chappell, V. C.: (ed.) *Hume – A Collection of Critical Essays*, Modern Studies in Philosophy, vol. II, London, 1968.

Church, R. W.: *Hume's Theory of the Understanding*, London, 1935.

Dewey, J.: *Experience and Nature*, London, 1929.

Düsing, K.: *Die Teleologie in Kants Weltbegriff*, Bonn, 1968.

Ehrlich, W.: *Kant und Husserl – Kritik der transzendentalen und phänomenologischen Methode*, Halle, 1923.

Friedmann, G.: *Psychologische Momente in der Ableitung des Apriori bei Kant, Versuch einer Versöhnung von Transzendentalismus und Kritischem Psychologismus*, Kant-Studien, Bd. XXV, 1921.

Green T. M. and Hudson, H. H.: (trans. with an introduction) *Kant's Religion Within the Limits of Reason Alone*, Chicago, Open Court Publishing Co., 1934.

Greig, J. Y. T.: (ed.) *The Letters of David Hume*, 2 vols., Oxford, 1932.

Groos, K.: *Hat Kant Humes Treatise gelesen?* Kant Studien, Bd. V, 1901.

Hasse, H.: *Das Problem der Gültigkeit in der Philosophie David Humes*, München, 1919.

Hedenius, I.: *Studies in Hume's Ethics*, Upsala/Stockholm, 1937.

Hedvall, K.: *Humes Erkenntnistheorie, kritisch dargestellt*, Upsala, 1906.

Heimsoeth, H.: *Astronomisches und Theologisches in Kants Weltverständnis*, Mainz, 1963.

—: *Die sechs grossen Themen der abendländischen Metaphysik*, Köln, 1965.

—: *Transszendentale Dialektik-Ein Kommentar zu Kants Kritik der reinen Vernunft*
   Berlin, 1966.
Hendel, C. W.: *Studies in the Philosophy of David Hume*, New York, 1963.
Huxley, T. H.: *Hume*, London, 1879.
James, W.: *The Varieties of Religious Experience – A Study in Human Nature*,
   Edinburgh, 1901–2.
—: *The Will to believe and other Essays in Popular Philosophy*, Longmans, Green
   & Co., London.
Kaulbach, F.: "Die Entwicklung des Synthesis-Gedankens bei Kant," in *Studien
   zu Kants philosophischer Entwicklung*, Bd. 6.
Kibéd, A. V. v.: *Macht und Ohnmacht der Vernunft – Zur Einführung in die
   Philosophie Kants*, München, 1967.
Körner, S.: *Kant*, A Pelican Book, London.
Krauser, P.: *Kritik der endlichen Vernunft – Diltheys Revolution der allgemeinen
   Wissenschafts- und Handlungstheorie*, Frankfurt a. M., 1968.
Kreis, F.: *Phänomenologie und Kritizismus*, Tübingen, 1930.
Kuypers, M. S.: *Studies in the Eighteenth Century Background of Hume's Empiri-
   cism*, Minneapolis, 1930.
Kydd, R.: *Reason and Conduct in Hume's Treatise*, London, 1946.
Laing, B. M.: *David Hume*, London, 1932.
Laird, J.: *Hume's Philosophy of Human Nature*, London, 1932.
Langen, Th.: *Morleau-Ponty's Critique of Reason*, London, 1966.
Leroy, A.: *La critique et la religion chez David Hume*, Paris, 1931.
Lorenz, K.: *Die Rückseite des Spiegels – Versuch einer Naturgeschichte mensch-
   lichen Erkennens*, R. Piper & Co. Verlag, München/Zürich, 1973.
Lovejoy, A. O.: *Reflections on Human Nature*, London, 1969.
MacNabb, D. I. C.: *David Hume – His Theory of Knowledge and Morality*, Hut-
   chinson's Univ. Library, 1951.
Madhava: *Sarva-darsana-samgraha*, Calcutta, 1889.
Mall, R. A.: *Experience and Reason*, The Hague, Martinus Nijhoff, 1973.
—: *Hume's Concept of Man – An Essay in Philosophical Anthropology*, Calcutta/
   London/New York, 1967.
—: *"Humes Prinzipien- und Kants Kategoriensystem,"* in Kant-Studien, Heft 3,
   1971.
—: "Husserl's Criticism of Kant's Theory of Knowledge," in *The Journal of the
   Indian Academy of Philosophy*, vol. 1, 1967.
—: "Naturalismus und Kritizismus – Hume und Kant" in *Akten des 4. Interna-
   tionalen Kant-Kongresses*, Mainz (West Germany), Teil II, 1, 1974.
Maund, C.: *Hume's Theory of Knowledge*, London, 1937.
Meinong, A.: *Hume-Studien*, Vienna, 1882.
Metz, R.: *David Hume – Leben und Philosophie*, Stuttgart, 1929.
Naess, A.: *Scepticism*, London, 1969.
Passmore, J. A.: *Hume's Intentions*, London, 1952.
Paton, H. J.: *The Categorical Imperative*, University of Chicago Press, 1948.
—: *Kant's Metaphysics of Experience*, 2 vols., London, Macmillan, 1936
Paulsen, F : *Immanuel Kant: His Life and Doctrine*, trans. by J. E. Creighton
   and A. Lefevre, New York, 1902.
Pitte, F. P. Van De: *Kant As Philosophical Anthropologist*, The Hague, Martinus
   Nijhoff, 1971.
Pölitz, K. H. L.: (ed.) *Vorlesungen über philosophische Religionslehre*, Leipzig,
   Carl Friedrich Frans, 1817.
Popkin, R.: "David Hume – His Pyrrhonism and his Critique of Pyrrhonism,"
   The Philosophical Quarterly, vol. I, no. 5, 1951.

—: "The Skeptical Precursors of David Hume," in *Philosophy and Phenomenological Research*, vol. XIV, 1954.

Popper, K.: *Conjectures and Refutations – The Growth of Scientific Knowledge*, London, 1965.

Price, H. H.: *Belief*, London, Allen & Unwin Ltd., 1969.

—: *Hume's Theory of the External World*, Oxford, 1963.

Radhakrishnan, S.: (ed., trans. with an introduction and commentary) *The Bhagavadgita*, London, Allen & Unwin Ltd.

—: *Indian Philosophy*, 2 vols., London, Allen & Unwin Ltd.

Reinach, A.: "Kants Auffassung des Humeschen Problems," in *Gesammelten Schriften*, ed. by Pupils, Halle, 1921.

Rescher, N.: "Kant and the 'Special Constitution' of Man's Mind: The Ultimately Factual basis of the Necessity and Universality of A Priori Synthetic Truths in Kant's Critical Philosophy," in *Akten des 4. Internationalen Kant-Kongresses*, Mainz, Teil II, 1, 1974.

Richter, P.: *Der Skeptizismus und seine Überwindung*, 2 vols., Leipzig, 1908.

Robson, J. W.: "Whitehead's Answer to Hume," in *Journal of Philosophy*, vol. XXXVIII, no. 4, 1941.

Rosenkranz, K. and Schubert, F. W.: (eds.) *Immanuel Kants Sämtliche Werke*, 12 vols., Leipzig, Leopold Voss, 1838–42.

Ross, W. D.: *Human Nature and Utility in Hume's Social Philosophy*, Berea, Ky., 1942.

Russel, B.: *History of Western Philosophy*, London, 1961.

Salmon, C. V.: *The Central Problem of David Hume's Philosophy*, Halle, 1929.

Sauer, F.: *Über das Verhältnis der Husserlschen Phänomenologie zu David Hume*, Kant-Studien, vol. XXXV.

Schaefer, A.: *David Hume – Philosophie und Politik*, Meisenheim am Glan, Anton Hain K.G., 1963.

Schiller, F. C. S.: "Humism and Humanism" in his book *Humanism*, New York, 1912.

Schilpp, P.: *Kant's Pre-Critical Ethics*, Evanston, Il., Northwestern University, 1938.

Schipper, E. W.: *Kant's Answer to Hume's Problem*, Kant-Studien, Bd. 53, 1961/62.

Schöndörfer, O.: *Immanuel Kant – Briefwechsel*, 2 vols., Leipzig, 1924.

Shearer, E. A.: *Hume's Place in Ethics*, Bryn Mawr, Pa., 1915.

Simmel, G.: *Kant*, München, 1924.

Smith, N. K.: *A Commentary to Kant's Critique of Pure Reason*, New York, Humanities Press, 1962.

—: (ed. with an introduction) *Hume's Dialogues Concerning Natural Religion*, London, 1947.

—: "The Naturalism of Hume," in *Mind*, vol. XIV, 1905.

—: *The Philosophy of David Hume*, London, 1960.

Starke, Fr. Ch.: *I. Kants Menschenkunde oder philosophische Anthropologie*, Leipzig, 1831.

Stephen, L.: *History of English Thought in the Eighteenth Century*, London, 1876.

Stewart, J. B.: *The Moral and Political Philosophy of David Hume*, New York, 1963.

Stuckenberg, J. W. H.: *The Life of Immanuel Kant*, London, 1882.

Tonelli, G.: *Die Anfänge von Kants Kritik der Kausalbeziehungen und ihre Voraussetzung im 18. Jahrhundert*, Kant-Studien, LVII, 1966.

—: "Kant und die antiken Skeptiker," in *Studien zu Kant's philosophischer Entwicklung*, Bd. 6.

Vaihinger, H.: *Die Philosophie des Als Ob*, Leipzig, 1920.
—: *Die Philosophie des Als Ob und das Kantische System gegenüber einem Erneurer des Atheismusstreites*, Kant-Studien, XXI, 1917.
Vleeschauwer, H.-J. D.: *The Development of Kantian Thought*, trans. by A. R. C. Duncan, London, 1962.
Vorländer, K.: *Immanuel Kants Leben*, Leipzig, 1921.
Walsh, W. H.: *Reason and Experience*, Oxford, 1947.
Warnock, G. J.: *Every Event has a Cause*, in Language and Logic Series, II.
Will, F. L.: *Will the Future be like the Past?* in Language and Logic Series, II.
Willey, B.: *The Eighteenth Century Background*, London, 1946.
Willich, A. F. M.: *Elements of the Critical Philosophy*, London, 1798.
Willy, M. L.: *The Subtle Knot – Creative Scepticism in XVIIth Century England*, London, 1952.
Wolf, R. P.: (ed.) *Kant – A Collection of Critical Essays*, Modern Studies in Philosophy, London, 1968.
—: *Kant's Theory of Mental Activity – A Commentary on the Transcendental Analytic of the Critique of Pure Reason*, Cambridge, 1963.
Yolton, J. W.: "The Concept of Experience in Locke and Hume," in *Journal of the History of Philosophy*, 1963.
Zweig, A.: (ed. and trans.) *Kant: Philosophical Correspondence 1759–99*, The University of Chicago Press, 1967.